JOURNAL FOR THE STUDY OF THE OLD TESTAMENT
SUPPLEMENT SERIES
201

Sheffield Academic Press

The Bible
and Criticism in
Victorian Britain

Profiles of F.D. Maurice
and William Robertson Smith

J.W. Rogerson

Journal for the Study of the Old Testament
Supplement Series 201

Copyright © 1995 Sheffield Academic Press

Published by Sheffield Academic Press Ltd
Mansion House
19 Kingfield Road
Sheffield, S11 9AS
England

Printed on acid-free paper in Great Britain
by Bookcraft
Midsomer Norton, Somerset

British Library Cataloguing in Publication Data

A catalogue record for this book is available
from the British Library

ISBN 1-85075-553-1

CONTENTS

LIST OF ABBREVIATIONS

AB	Anchor Bible
BFE	*British and Foreign Evangelical Review*
BQR	*British Quarterly Review*
BZAW	Beihefte zur *ZAW*
FOTL	The Forms of the Old Testament Literature
HAT	Handbuch zum Alten Testament
JSOTSup	*Journal for the Study of the Old Testament*, Supplement Series
Numen	*Numen: International Review for the History of Religions*
SBT	Studies in Biblical Theology
TRE	*Theologische Realenzyklopädie*
ZAW	*Zeitschrift für die alttestamentliche Wissenschaft*

INTRODUCTION

> Gegensätze und Widersprüche gehören überhaupt zur geistigen Lebendigkeit.[1]

In Oscar Wilde's *The Importance of Being Earnest* Lady Bracknell speaks the following memorable line: 'To lose one parent, Mr Worthing, may be regarded as a misfortune; to lose both looks like carelessness'.[2] This line has come to mind as I have reflected on the fact that, in recent years, I have spent much time studying scholars who were dismissed from their posts. W.M.L. de Wette, on whom I published a biography in 1992,[3] was dismissed from his post at the University of Berlin in 1819, while the two scholars who are treated in the present volume also lost their jobs (all three happily found other employment). F.D. Maurice was dismissed from King's College, London in 1854 and W. Robertson Smith lost his chair at the Free Church College in Aberdeen in 1881. What Lady Bracknell would have said about my predilection for dismissed scholars must remain speculation; but if she had observed that it was not entirely carelessness she would have been correct. For while I have never consciously made a decision to study scholars who lost their jobs at some point in their careers, I have found myself drawn to the type of scholar who was most likely to be dismissed, in those heady days before the churches decided to deal with the prophetic voices in their midst by simply ignoring them.

Although de Wette, Maurice and Smith were quite different from each other, what they shared in common was the conviction that the Bible had to be interpreted from the standpoint of the world in which they lived and worked. In de Wette's case the setting was the crisis of faith

---

1. W. Vatke, *Die biblische Theologie wissenschaftlich dargrstellt. I. Die Religion des Alten Testaments* (Berlin, 1835).

2. O. Wilde, *The Importance of Being Earnest: A Trivial Comedy for Serious People*, in R. Ross (ed.), *Works* (London: Methuen, 3rd edn, 1909), VII, p. 44.

3. J.W. Rogerson, *W.M.L. de Wette, Founder of Modern Biblical Criticism: An Intellectual Biography* (JSOTSup, 126; Sheffield: JSOT Press, 1992).

brought about by the use of historical criticism and the challenge of
Kantian philosophy, combined with the political upheavals in the German
states at the end of the Napoleonic wars. Maurice was responding to the
rapid industrialization of Britain in the mid-nineteenth century and to the
attempts of the Church of England to recover its role as the national
church. Smith lived through the most exciting period of modern biblical
studies and sought to bring the new biblical criticism as well as the
exploding amount of scientific and other knowledge of his day into the
service of theology. All three were bound to collide with ecclesiastical
authorities because, in their different ways, they saw that the received
orthodoxies of their respective traditions could not meet the needs of
their day.[4] This is one of the factors that makes them into figures of
abiding interest.

My own interest in Maurice and Smith would probably have
remained nothing more than that had I not been invited to give courses
of lectures which provided the opportunity for research and publication.
The invitation to give the F.D. Maurice Lectures at King's College,
London in 1992 was open-ended, but since, as far as I was aware, there
was no treatment anywhere of Maurice as an interpreter of the Old
Testament, I decided to devote the three Maurice lectures to that theme.
I am grateful to the Maurice trustees for the invitation and to Professor
Michael Knibb for arranging excellent hospitality on the occasion of
their delivery.

The lectures on Smith were specifically requested. Some years ahead
of the 1994 centenary of Smith's death, Professor William Johnstone of
Aberdeen began to ensure that the occasion would not pass unnoticed.
The result of his hard work was an outstandingly successful international
Congress in Aberdeen in April 1994, whose proceedings will be
published in 1995.[5] My own contribution to that Congress also appears
as Chapter 10 in the present volume, for the sake of completeness and
with Professor Johnstone's permission. However, 1994 saw not only the

---

4.   De Wette was dismissed, officially, on political grounds, for writing a letter of
sympathy to the mother of a theological student who had carried out a political
assassination. But he had been a marked man because of his advanced theological
views, and theological considerations affected the political decisions that led to his
dismissal. See further my *W.M.L. de Wette*, pp. 145-58 n. 2.

5.   W. Johnstone (ed.), *William Robertson Smith: Essays in Reassessment:
Proceedings of the Robertson Smith Congress, Aberdeen 5–9 April 1994* (Sheffield:
JSOT Press, forthcoming).

centenary of Smith's death but also the beginnings of the quincentenary celebrations of the University of Aberdeen in 1995. The trustees of the Gifford Lectures decided to arrange five series of six lectures on aspects of the intellectual life of Scotland during the period 1495–1995, and I was asked to deliver six Gifford Lectures on Smith. This I did in April–May 1994 under the title 'Criticism and Faith in the work of William Robertson Smith'. I am most grateful to the Principal of the University of Aberdeen for the invitation and to Professor William and Dr Elizabeth Johnstone for many kindnesses during my visits to Aberdeen.

On the assumption that there may be readers who are unfamiliar with the careers of Maurice and Smith I shall outline them briefly, together with some general observations by way of introduction to the lectures. Maurice was born in 1805, the son of a Unitarian minister who was orthodox and non-subscribing.[6] The household was not free from religious strife, with Maurice's mother and sister embracing forms of Calvinism. Maurice also abandoned Unitarianism, although after studying law at Cambridge he still felt sufficiently strongly about subscribing to the Articles of Religion of the Church of England that he declined to be a candidate for a college fellowship. However, in 1830 he went to Oxford with a view to being ordained in the Church of England, and following ordination and a curacy he was Chaplain at Guy's Hospital, London, before being appointed in 1840 to a professorship in English literature and history at the recently founded Church of England King's College, London. In 1846 he was elected to be Chaplain at Lincoln's Inn and in 1848 he was involved in founding Queen's College, a pioneering institution for higher education for women. Maurice's increasing involvement with Christian Socialism made him suspect in some quarters, and in 1853 he was obliged to resign from his post at King's College because of his view, expressed in his *Theological Essays* (1853), that punishment in hell was not everlasting.[7] His resignation at Lincoln's Inn

6.   By way of over-simplification it can be said that two types of unitarianism had emerged, partly out of English Presbyterianism, by the beginning of the nineteenth century. One type was mostly orthodox in belief but refused to be bound by subscription to the traditional dogmatic and credal formulae of the church. In some cases the New Testament was appealed to in support of this position. If the confession 'Jesus is Lord' sufficed for admission to the church in New Testament times, why should more be required now? The other type, which most people associate with Unitarianism, was subordinationist in its Christology and universalist in outlook.

7.   For further details see F. Maurice, *The Life of Frederick Dennison Maurice chiefly told in his own letters* (London, 1884), II, pp. 163-209.

was refused, and he continued his Chaplaincy until 1860, when he became Chaplain at St Peter's, Vere Street in London. In 1866 he became Professor of Moral Theology and Philosophy at Cambridge, which post he combined with the Vere Street Chaplaincy, until ill health forced him to resign from the latter in 1869. He died in 1872.

Smith's dismissal from the Free Church College in Aberdeen in 1881 affected his life radically. The work that he fell back upon initially was editing the ninth edition of the *Encyclopaedia Britannica*, and this task occupied him for many more years. However, in 1883 he removed to Cambridge where he remained for the rest of his short life, occupying posts as University Librarian and Professor of Arabic. Like Maurice, Smith was a son of the manse, in this case that of the Free Church minister and schoolmaster in Keig near Aberdeen. When Smith was born in 1846 it was only three years since hundreds of ministers and elders had left the Church of Scotland to form a Free Church, free from interference from secular patrons and civil courts of law. This great movement entailed the building of new churches, schools and colleges and it was in the Free Church's college in Aberdeen that Smith taught from 1870–1881.

His dismissal resulted mainly from the publication of the pioneering article 'Bible' in the ninth edition of the *Encyclopaedia Britannica* in 1875. This article is discussed fully in Chapter 6. Proceedings against Smith in the college, the Presbytery and the General Assembly lasted from 1876 to 1881, with the cruel twist that he was acquitted and admonished in May 1880 only to be suspended a matter of weeks later and dismissed the following year on account of two further articles that were in the press at the time of his acquittal.[8] Smith's education and theological formation are described in Chapter 5.

Of the two men, I have a much clearer impression of Smith than of Maurice, probably because he was a larger than life character. He was a brilliant linguist. As a student he could already read German and Dutch and he became a master of colloquial and literary Arabic. This was in addition, of course, to Hebrew and the classical languages. He was a great traveller—to the continent of Europe, Egypt and the Arabian peninsular. His coverage of subjects was phenomenal, for not only could he have had an academic career in mathematics or physics had he wished, his Old Testament and Arabian studies led him into the field of

---

8.   The trials are described fully in J.S. Black and G. Chrystal, *The Life of William Robertson Smith* (London: A. & C. Black, 1912).

social anthropology and sociology where his work had an immediate impact. His ties with scholars in all parts of the world were probably unmatched in his lifetime. Partly, this came from his work for the *Encyclopaedia Britannica*, but also from his interest and expertise in so many fields. Although the Cambridge University Library archive contains a vast collection of his letters (and of letters to him) it is evident that there are also Smith letters in archives in Holland, Germany and North America. Their addition to the Cambridge collection as photocopies is an urgent task for the future.[9]

In spite of this enormous erudition and thirst for knowledge, and his removal from theology to Arabian Studies, Smith remained a theologian, and one of the aims of the lectures that are presented here is to give an account of Smith as a theologian. Further, in preparing the lectures I have become aware of the extent to which Smith was a contributor to the development of biblical criticism and not, as his critics often alleged, merely a purveyor of others' ideas. I have tried to show how Smith combined a willingness to embrace quite radical critical theories with an evangelical faith that was convinced to the last that the Old Testament contained a divine revelation.

If Smith was a man riding the crest of the new wave of biblical criticism, Maurice was essentially a transitional figure, ready to be open to moderate criticism but scandalized by the first hints of the radical implications of criticism. If Smith was the great international figure, Maurice concentrated on matters closer at home; and good matters they were too. He was a pioneer in the education of women and working-class men. He was involved in setting up trades associations to protect workers and provide them with decent working conditions. He was a trusted adviser to workers' leaders. He stood for a view of religion that refused to see it compartmentalized or restricted to an area marked 'sacred'; he wanted religion to inform all human activity. In this respect he and Smith stood close together, and it is this aspect of Maurice's work that I have tried to explore in my lectures.

The lectures that follow are printed as they were written for oral delivery, which is why each tries to end with a punch line designed to tempt listeners back for the next session. As such, they cannot pretend to be exhaustive treatments.

Among the people that I wish to thank are Dr F.W. Ratcliffe, recently

9. The Cambridge University Archive contains scores of letters relating to Smith's editorial work for the *Encyclopaedia Britannica*.

retired as the Cambridge University Librarian, for permission to use the Smith archive, and for his hospitality. Generous hospitality was also provided by Professor J.A. Emerton on my visits to Cambridge, while Professor R.E. Clements provided many kindnesses both at King's College, London and in Cambridge. During my current brief visit to Göttingen I have had the opportunity to discuss Smith's relationship with Wellhausen and Lagarde with Professor Rudolf Smend, for whose insights and suggestions I am always grateful. My final thanks go to my wife Rosalind, and to Gill Fogg and Janet Needham in the Sheffield Department of Biblical Studies, all of whom have assisted in the typing and formatting of the lectures.

J.W. Rogerson
Göttingen, November 1994

Part I

F.D. MAURICE AS INTERPRETER OF THE OLD TESTAMENT:
THE F.D. MAURICE LECTURES FOR 1992

Chapter 1

ORDER AND CREATION IN THE OLD TESTAMENT

Maurice's treatment of the Old Testament was mainly confined to sermons. The two volumes of sermons entitled *Patriarchs and Lawgivers of the Old Testament* and *Prophets and Kings of the Old Testament* contain 46 sermons preached at Lincoln's Inn between 16 February 1851 and 20 June 1852. To these can be added a further six sermons on Old Testament subjects in *The Doctrine or Sacrifice deduced from the Scriptures* which were preached at Lincoln's Inn from 26 February to 30 April 1854. In addition, some of the sermons given at Lincoln's Inn from 3 December 1848 which were published under the title *The Prayer Book* contain addresses on the Old Testament; and we must not overlook the sections on the Old Testament in Maurice's best known works *The Kingdom of Christ* and *Theological Essays*.[1] This list of sources is not exhaustive;[2] but it is a sufficiently large sample to ensure an adequate coverage of Maurice's handling of the Old Testament. As far as I can judge, Maurice's view of the Old Testament did not develop once he had established his mature convictions. His sermons on the Old Testament were thus a dialogue between the text and his beliefs. This dialogue inevitably repeated Maurice's basic convictions; but it was almost always fresh and vigorous and driven by the belief that the Old Testament lessons read at divine service were meant to speak to himself and his listeners. I shall deal with this last point later in the first lecture;

---

1.   F.D. Maurice, *The Patriarchs and Lawgivers of the Old Testament* (London, 1892); *The Prophets and Kings of the Old Testament* (London, 1879); *The Doctrine of Sacrifice Deduced from the Scriptures* (Cambridge, 1854); *The Prayer Book* (London: James Clarke, 3rd edn, 1966); *The Kingdom of Christ* (2 vols.; repr.; London: James Clarke, 2nd edn, 1959 [1842]); *Theological Essays* (Cambridge, 1853).

2.   There are a few resources on the Old Testament in *Lincoln's Inn Sermons* (6 vols.; London, 1891–92).

but in order to indicate the nature of Maurice's style, I shall quote some sentences from his sermon on the purpose of the Old Testament lesson from his series on the *Prayer Book*:

> The word 'Lesson' implies that we are not speaking but spoken to. Another is teaching; we sit to learn. Now thoughts of this kind suggest themselves to a great many in every Church where the Old Testament is read, 'What have we to do with these? We have been hearing perhaps a Chapter out of the Book of Kings, perhaps one of Jewish Prophecy—the first is simple enough, but it belongs to the far-gone past; the other, for aught we know, may belong to past, present or future, but we do not understand it. We can find something profitable to our souls in the Psalms...The commandments we admit are of standing value but why not make a collection of profitable extracts; why force upon an English congregation, composed of the most various elements, that which cannot be applicable to the condition of one in twenty?'[3]

Maurice answered his rhetorical questions as follows:

> 'Sit down' says the Prayer-Book, 'and listen. Hear this Chapter, and this. We tell you it is a lesson. We tell you that it will interpret yourselves to you and the world to you. And again, that the world and yourselves, or, in other words, God's dealings with the world and yourselves will interpret *it* to you.'[4]

Incidentally, Maurice by no means confined his preaching to the lessons prescribed for Sundays in the Book of Common Prayer. His addresses in *Patriarchs and Lawgivers* did follow the appointed readings from Septuagesima to the Third Sunday after Trinity in 1851; but this was not an invariable practice. It must also be said that Maurice did not go through passages verse by verse in his sermons. Rather, he would concentrate on one or two main ideas in a passage, and enlarge and elaborate them. This method inevitably left many questions unanswered.

The two main ideas that inform Maurice's use of the Old Testament are these: first, the Bible is the record of God's dealings with the human race. In these dealings, God seeks to educate humanity so that it learns the moral principle on which the universe is based, and comes to accept and live by this principle. Thus, the Bible is not a set of teachings or doctrines about God. Nor is it a law book containing God's moral instructions to the human race. It is the story of God dealing with men and women, and men and women who are not particularly special or

---

3. *The Prayer Book*, p. 71.
4. *The Prayer Book*, p. 74.

even particularly religious. In these dealings, which include punishments to guide and correct his people, God shows who he is and what he requires. The value of the Old Testament for readers in Maurice's days is that its stories will help them to see that the same God wishes to have dealings with them *now*, who had dealings with people *then* in the sacred stories.

The second main idea behind Maurice's approach to the Old Testament is that God's purpose is to bless and to accept the whole human race. Maurice totally rejected any idea of the Fall that implied that the human race stood under the judgment of God so that only a small elect would be saved from hell. He also rejected the view that Christ had died only for those predestined to be saved. Further, Christ's death had not been a sacrifice which reconciled God to humanity and now made it possible for God to forgive the human race. The death of Christ had been part of God's reaching out in love to the human race, and it created new possibilities for humanity, new possibilities into which men and women were to be invited. One of Maurice's most perceptive modern inter-preters, H.G. Wood, suggests that Maurice would have agreed with the scholastic theologians who believed that the Incarnation would have taken place even if there had been no fall of the human race. 'The Son of God became Son of Man, for us men as well as for our salvation'. [5]

In showing how these main ideas were applied to the Old Testament, I begin with Maurice's sermons on the Creation and the Fall. In the sermon on Creation (the text chosen is Gen. 2.1) Maurice argues that Genesis 1–2 does not allude to the creation of the material universe:

> Scriptural readers and commentators have insisted that the Mosaic history
> of Creation shall be the history of the formation of the material earth,
> though there is not a single sentence in which the slightest allusion is made
> to that formation.[6]

Maurice goes on to say that this position means that there will be no clash between his interpretation of Genesis 1–2 and the findings of modern science; but he is at pains to emphasize that this is not the reason why he adopts the position that he does:

---

5.   H.G. Wood, *Frederick Denison Maurice* (Cambridge: Cambridge University Press, 1950), p. 112.

6.   *Patriarchs and Lawgivers*, pp. 43-44.

We have the greatest interest in getting rid of them [notions that Gen. 1–2 is about the creation of the material world]—not in order to make peace with science, not even in order to assert the letter of Scripture, though both these objects are highly important,—but because, as long as these conceptions last, we cannot enter into that idea of Creation which the Scripture is in every page bringing out before us; because we cannot feel the beauty of that order of the Universe which Moses was permitted to reveal to us.[7]

These last words bring us to the heart of Maurice's understanding of the purpose of Genesis 1–2. God somehow communicated to Moses a vision of the universe seen from the divine point of view. It was a universe still in the process of becoming (note the command to the earth to produce grass and to the trees and vegetation to produce seed and to the animals to be fruitful and multiply—something that they were still doing); but if it was a universe still in process of becoming it was complete in the sense that it perfectly represented what was in the mind of God; and it was what was in the mind of God that Genesis 1–2 was intended to convey, so that the reader gained not information about how the world came into being, but an awareness of a Being 'who is, and was, and is to come'.

The purpose of Genesis 1–2 was to deliver the human race from idolatry, which for Maurice meant the worship of the creature instead of the creator. The six-day scheme of creation was designed to make the readers contemplate the order of the universe so that they would know that they were not the rulers of the universe. The command to rest on the seventh day was a further reminder that human beings were not the rulers of creation and was also, and more importantly, a way of discovering how to live in harmony with the order that was at the heart of creation.

The most striking thing about Maurice's sermon on the Fall is his insistence that there is no difference between what Adam did once and what we do now. The offence of Adam and Eve was that they declined to be dependent upon God and insisted on becoming independent. As Maurice put it: 'they claimed to be something which they were not. They refused to be that which they were'.[8] Adam and Eve wanted to be gods, not to be in the image of God. They wished to above the law, not subject to it. The fact that we, today, can match this from our own experience confirms the truth of the Old Testament story.

7.   *Patriarchs and Lawgivers*, p. 44.
8.   *Patriarchs and Lawgivers*, p. 54.

What, then, were the consequences of the Fall? The first was the coming of death, by which Maurice seems to mean that God let Adam and Eve have their own way. If they wished to be independent beings, then they would suffer the same fate as other animals. The second consequence was that they were driven from their garden into a harsh world where the ground was cursed and brought forth thorns and thistles. Yet, if this seemed to be a punishment, it was also a blessing. The disobedience of Adam and Eve did not destroy or undermine God's order. Rather, it created the situation in which the human race could now learn more about God's order; learn how it was possible to be human and inhuman; how it was possible to try to frustrate the purposes of God and how it was possible to live in harmony with them.

The Fall, then, set in motion a process of divine education of the human race, an education of which the Bible was the record. The God of this process was not the stern God of Calvinism condemning all humanity except the elect to eternal torment on account of Adam's sin. It was a God striving with the whole human race, seeking to make humans right within. This did not mean that God was a benevolent parent indifferent to human wrongdoings. There was judgment, and there was punishment brought about by God. But this was God 'carrying on a perpetual course of discipline for [the] reformation and restoration [of the human race]'.[9] Towards the end of the sermon on the Fall is a passage which sums up Maurice's view of the Old Testament, his approach to the problem of evil, and his conception of the nature and purposes of God. Answering the question why God could not purge the world and humanity from their corruptions by a fiat of omnipotence, Maurice replied:

> Because...He had made man in his own image; because He had given him a Will; because He could only restore and regenerate him by restoring and regenerating his Will. Hence we have to read all the Bible through, of floods, famines, pestilences, earthquakes, anarchy, tyranny. It is throughout the history of an actual government,—throughout, the history of an actual education; a government of voluntary creatures to teach them subjection;— an education of voluntary creatures to make them free. And He who carries on this government and education, is seen, the more He makes Himself known to us, to be not a hard despot, but a loving Ruler; with that heart and sympathy in perfection which He requires in His creatures.[10]

9. *Patriarchs and Lawgivers*, p. 62.
10. *Patriarchs and Lawgivers*, p. 63.

So far, I have dealt with that part of the lecture which uses the word 'order'. I now turn to consider Maurice's use of the notion of covenant, something that brings us to Maurice's treatment of the history of Israel.

In a sermon preached on Whit Sunday, 8 June 1851, Maurice departed from the set lessons and chose his text from Deut. 30.19-20. He described Deuteronomy as a constitutional treatise, as a statement of the fundamental principles which determined the existence of Israel as the people of God. Most basic of all these principles was the *fact* of a redemption already received. It was stated early in Deuteronomy when the reason for observing the Sabbath commandment was linked to the exodus from Egypt; but it was implied throughout Deuteronomy by the repetition of the words 'thou shalt remember that thou wast a bondman in Egypt'. In Maurice's own words:

> That fact of redemption lay…beneath all the institutions which the chosen people were enjoined to preserve. Apart from the faith and acknowledgement of it, their institutions,—one and all,—became unreal, unintelligible. They could not observe them, if they did not receive them as witnesses that they had been delivered from a tyrant and taken under God's immediate government. That truth was the foundation of their society. It would hold together so long as that truth was remembered. It would perish when that truth was lost.[11]

Granted this statement, it does not require much imagination to see how Maurice preached his way through the historical and prophetic books of the Old Testament. The history of the people of the covenant was the history of a nation continually asked to choose between life and death; between life which God had already made possible and which was enjoyed by living in obedience to him, and death which was not God's will, but which inevitably followed when Israel foresook God and tried to live without him. Yet even when Israel chose death, which seems to have been most of the time, the nation was not out of reach of God's mercy and forgiveness. According to Maurice, the book of Deuteronomy presumes that the Israelites have incurred the deepest curse which the book pronounces, but it still addresses them as children of the covenant, and states that God is at hand to lift them from the abyss of unbelief and falsehood into which they have sunk. Commenting on the clause in the Ten Commandments that God is a jealous God who punishes the sins of the fathers to the third and fourth generations Maurice declares:

11. *Patriarchs and Lawgivers*, p. 290.

> There is a jealous God, jealous over his creatures because He loves
> them,—who is watching over them when they are wandering furthest from
> Him...He has not caused or decreed their superstitions, their divisions,
> their slavery. All have come from their not choosing the state which He
> intended for them; from their going out of the good way, from their liking
> death better than life.[12]

And in an illuminating comment on this observation, Maurice says that
what he calls ordinary history cannot tell us how people who are sinking
deeper and deeper into the abyss of their own choosing can be rescued
from it. This, he declares, 'is precisely the information which the Scriptures are written to give us; that ordinary history may become to us not
a dark but an illuminated scroll'.[13]

Among the institutions of the covenant with Israel were the provisions
for sacrifice, and it is to these that I now turn. Maurice's treatment of
sacrifice is interesting in itself, and it is also a useful way of approaching
how Maurice believed that the Old Testament addressed the society of
his own day.

Maurice's most profound treatment of sacrifice in the Old Testament is
not, as we might expect, in the sermons on sacrifice, but in two sermons
preached on Easter Day, 22 April 1851, and the following Sunday.[14]
The first, entitled 'The Passover' and based loosely on the evening
reading, Exodus 14, connected the institution of sacrifice with the
Passover, and not, as we might have expected, with the law-giving at
Sinai. The connection of sacrifice with the Passover and the deliverance
from slavery in Egypt enabled Maurice to argue that sacrifices
symbolized and effected the return of people to an orderly state of
affairs that had been disrupted.

As slaves in Egypt, the proper status and position of the Israelites had
been degraded from what they should have been. On the eve of their
deliverance they are to kill a lamb and to daub the blood on the doors of
their tents. This action is a witness to the Pharaoh that the Hebrew
slaves are about to be restored to their proper status as the redeemed
people of God. Thus, sacrifices in ancient Israel are an order or system
whose purpose is to declare that the Israelites are a called and sanctified

---

12. *Patriarchs and Lawgivers*, p. 300.
13. *Patriarchs and Lawgivers*, p. 301. We can suggest that Maurice's view is
similar to that in Augustine's *City of God*: that the history recorded in the Bible
shows us the reality beyond all history.
14. See *Patriarchs and Lawgivers*, pp. 186-203 and 204-20.

people. Sacrifices are not offerings to win God's favour or to change his mind. They embody a vital principle. Since sacrifices involve the surrender of something valuable on the part of those who make them, they indicate the truth that, in order to restore what has been disturbed, the giving up of something is involved. In the case of human behaviour, order is disrupted when humans assert their own rules in opposition to the will of God. Order is restored when that human self-will is given up. Sacrifices proclaim and embody the need for self-surrender if order is to replace disruption.

But sacrifice in the Old Testament requires a priesthood, and it is in his discussion of priesthood on 27 May 1851 that Maurice makes one of his strongest connections between the Old Testament and the society of his own day. One of the lessons for the day was Numbers 16, the rebellion of Korah, Dathan, Abiram and others against the authority of Moses and Aaron. Maurice points out that Korah was a Levite and that the protest was not, therefore, the protest of lay people against the existence of the priestly order, but a protest about the nature of priestly authority itself. This led Maurice to reflect upon the purposes of the priesthood, and upon its possible abuses.

An important part of this reflection is a distinction between priesthood as an order and priesthood as a caste. A caste, according to Maurice, is a group that is jealous of its own privileges, power and prestige, a group that believes that it possesses the right to pass on to others the privilege of membership, a group that is concerned to protect its position from invasion from without. An order, on the other hand, acknowledges that God is the giver of its privileges, and that God is able to withdraw these privileges at any time if the order becomes concerned with its own existence, and forgets that it is there to assist in God's purposes.

Maurice claims that priesthood, which is an order ordained by God, contains the tendency to become a caste; and he warns himself and his fellow-clergy against overstepping the limits of the order to which God has called them:

> We who minister in holy things should remember of what infinite confu-
> sion we may be the cause, through our pride and self-exultation, through
> our eager assertion of rights and powers, when our business is to confess
> responsibilities; through our fancy that we are doing God service by

lifting up ourselves above civil rulers, by complaining of our ecclesiastical
superiors, by feverish and restless efforts to get a position for ourselves
which God has not given us.[15]

But it is far too soon for hard-pressed politicians and archdeacons to
cheer Maurice's apparent attempt to keep the lower clergy in their
place. He now switches his argument by noting that, if Korah was a
Levite, some of those who supported his rebellion were laypeople. By
insisting that they, too, should have a share in priestly ministry they
were supporting the lie, a lie all too often encouraged by priests, that
only priests are consecrated to the service of God. At this point, Maurice
needs to be quoted again.

> We [clergy] are sent into the world in this day, as the tribe of Levi was sent
> into the world under the old dispensation, to bear witness for the consecra-
> tion and the holiness of God's entire family. We become guilty, as they
> did, when by our words or acts we lead you to think that you have not
> received this consecration; that you are not set apart to God; that you and
> your children and your occupations are not holy in His sight.[16]

In other words, priests in ancient Israel existed to symbolize and effect
the consecration of every aspect of human life; and what was true for
ancient Israel was also true for Christian ministers today. Christian clergy
exist to symbolize and effect the truths, first, that all human life is based
upon sacrifice—the surrender of self-will—and secondly, that all human
life is under the rule of God who is the 'real ground of its orders and
institutions'. Thus it is the duty of clergy to proclaim that every aspect
of human life is subject to God's laws and part of his purposes, even to
the point where this brings them into collision with prominent men in
civic and ecclesiastical life. To quote Maurice again:

> Let him [the priest] make the people who are living under it [local or
> central government] see that...their society is no work of human hands, no
> result of vulgar conventions. Let him say further, that God being the author
> and lawgiver of human society, all its disorders and anomalies are contrary
> to His will; and that statesmen as well as churchmen, instead of tolerating
> and excusing them, ought to be labouring day and night for the removal of
> them...a man who takes this course may be very disagreeable to the high
> or the low wrong-doers of the land...but he will not and cannot be a
> disturber of the family or national order of a country.[17]

15. *Patriarchs and Lawgivers*, pp. 215-16.
16. *Patriarchs and Lawgivers*, p. 216.
17. *Patriarchs and Lawgivers*, pp. 218-19.

My initial exposition of Maurice's use of the Old Testament for his own society is almost complete. It needs to be rounded off by reference to the sermon delivered on 11 May 1851, the Third Sunday after Easter. The evening lesson was Deuteronomy 5, and Maurice took from it the words 'ye shall walk in all the ways which the Lord your God hath commanded you, that ye may live, and that it may be well with you, and that ye may prolong your days in the land that ye shall possess'. The sermon is a sustained attack on the view that the Old Testament differs from the New Testament because it is concerned with material blessings in this life, whereas the focus of the New Testament is upon spiritual, eternal benefits. The sermon contains so many memorable passages that the temptation to quote more than taste or time allow is considerable. Here is one such passage:

> It is surely a perilous and almost fatal notion, that Christian men have less to do with the present than the Jews had, that their minds and their religion are to be projected into a region after death, because there only the Divine Presence is dwelling. Is it possible that this is what the writers of the New Testament meant when they proclaimed that the Son of God had taken flesh and become man, and that thenceforth the Lord God would dwell with men and walk with them, and that they should be His children and He would be their Father? Do such words import, that the world in which God has placed us has lost some of the sacredness which it had before; that the visible has become hopelessly separated from the invisible; that earth and heaven are not as much united as they were when Jacob was travelling to the land of the people of the east; that now earth is merely a forlorn place, in which men are forced to stay a certain number of years, engaged in a number of occupations with which Heaven has nothing to do, while yet it is held that the preparation for Heaven is the great business of those who dwell here? Surely there must be a terrible contradiction in such language, a contradiction which cannot fail to exhibit itself in our practice, to introduce unreality, insincerity, heartlessness into every part of it.[18]

Maurice insisted, then, that the Old Testament was a vital text for the society of his day because it was the account of God's dealings with an entire nation and not the story of a specifically religious people. What Israel was to enjoy was a salvation in our material world, not a salvation in an afterworld. As Maurice was preaching, the shock-waves of the revolutions in Europe of 1848 were still being felt. Maurice referred to them in this sermon of May 1851, together with his own fear that the churches would try to prop up the existing order in Britain by making

18. *Patriarchs and Lawgivers*, p. 251-52.

common cause with the upper and middle classes against the working classes. The aim of this alliance would be to preserve the respective privileges of the church and what Maurice called the respectable classes. But for Maurice, this was a denial of the church's role to proclaim that all members of a nation were of concern to God, and that all activities were to be related to God's purposes. He believed that the nation was facing a choice between faith and atheism. Atheism would be the acceptance of the view that there is a separate, religious department in the affairs of the nation to which the things of God are to be confined. Faith would be the belief, and its practical consequences, that *all* the pursuits and toils and relations of *all* humans were of concern to God and that they were 'holy according to God's eternal order and purpose'. To quote a second of the memorable passages:

> If we believe in our hearts that the New Testament is not contrary to the Old; that our Covenant is larger, deeper, more social than the Jewish...that every maxim of trade or government, however sustained by custom, opinion, authority, which is opposed to Truth and Righteousness, is doomed to perish; then we have a Gospel which men will listen to in the nineteenth century more than they did in the sixteenth or the third.[19]

In this lecture I have tried to present Maurice as a powerful advocate of the message of the Old Testament for his own times. Those present who are familiar with Maurice's writings will no doubt feel, and with justification, that I have presented Maurice too positively: that I have overlooked his sometimes elusive and obscure style and that I have underestimated his deficiencies as a systematic thinker. There are, indeed, aspects of Maurice's Old Testament sermons that can irritate modern readers. In the sermon on the Fall, Maurice states that he believes that the devil tempted Adam, but he insists that the text says that it was a beast, not a spirit that tempted Adam, and that we should not try to improve upon Moses. In the *Theological Essays* where there is a discussion of the Evil Spirit, Maurice tells us nothing of his views about the origin of evil or the devil, but prefers to insist that God offers victory over the devil and his works.[20] Again, in the sermon on Balaam, the non-Israelite who was reproved by his donkey, Maurice treats the talking ass in a cavalier fashion. Whereas this remarkable talking animal had worried interpreters even as far back as the compilers of *Pirke*

---

19. *Patriarchs and Lawgivers*, p. 253-54.
20. *Theological Essays*, pp. 34-55.

Aboth 9, where Balaam's ass is a special creation in the interval between the close of the work of creation and the beginning of the very first Sabbath, Maurice was able to say:

> How '*the dumb ass rebuked the madness of the prophet*' I know not, nor care to know. But I believe that whatever sounds it uttered, they did convey exactly that meaning to the mind of the prophet which it is said that they conveyed.[21]

How does this naivety, as it seems to us, and others that can be adduced, affect our estimate of Maurice as an Old Testament interpreter? Was he a pre-critical user of the Old Testament? If so, can he have anything to say to us? The second lecture will address the matter of Maurice and biblical criticism, paving the way for a treatment in the third lecture of Maurice and contemporary issues.

21. *Patriarchs and Lawgivers*, p. 230.

Chapter 2

MAURICE AND THE OLD TESTAMENT CRITICISM OF HIS DAY

At the end of the first lecture in this series, I drew attention to some elements of Maurice's use of the Old Testament that at best slightly irritate, and at worst infuriate anyone familiar with historical-critical study of the Bible. In this second lecture I shall discuss four questions: (1) what was the state of Old Testament criticism in 1852? (2) How much did Maurice know about this historical criticism? (3) What were his own critical positions? (4) How and why did he react to *Essays and Reviews* in 1860 and to volume I of Colenso's *The Pentateuch and Joshua* in 1862?

1. *The State of Old Testament Criticism in 1852*

In 1852, three years after his death, the seventh edition of de Wette's *Lehrbuch der historisch-kritischen Einleitung in das Alte Testament* was published in Berlin.[1] This book had been regarded as the standard work of its type since the appearance of the first edition in 1817; and although de Wette had some views that were not widely shared, his Introduction can be taken as a benchmark for the state of historical-critical scholarship in the middle of the nineteenth century. The following is a summary of the positions set out by de Wette.[2]

The basis of the first four books of the Pentateuch is an epic and poetic narrative which uses the divine name 'Elohim' for God, and was known as the Elohim document. It combined what later scholarship distinguished as the 'E' source and the Priestly Code. It was written probably in the tenth century BCE after the division of the kingdom. Combined

1.   W.M.L. de Wette, *Lehrbuch der historisch-kritischen Einleitung in das Alte Testament* (Berlin, 7th edn, 1852).
2.   For more details on de Wette and his position see my *W.M.L. de Wette.*

with the Elohim document were parallel and supplementary narratives which used the name YHWH for God. When these narratives were isolated they had the appearance of fragments rather than self-contained narratives; but de Wette was prepared to allow that the J narratives had once been a complete source, which the Jehovist had inserted into the Elohim document. This had been done early in the eighth century BCE. The book of Deuteronomy had been written in the time of Josiah (640–609) and had been added later to the first four books of the Pentateuch. There was no possibility that Moses had written the Pentateuch, even if there were fragments in the sources older than their time of writing down.

The book of Joshua continued the Elohim document, but in its final form Deuteronomistic material had been added into Joshua, from which it followed that Joshua was composed probably in the seventh century. The same was true of Judges with its Deuteronomistic material; but de Wette was impressed with the living and natural characters of some of the stories in Judges, to which he was therefore prepared to ascribe an early date. The books of Samuel contained material that had a genuine historical ring (de Wette was thinking of the story of David's court in 2 Samuel). There were also parallel and duplicate narratives, especially in 1 Samuel. The final form presupposed a Deuteronomistic redaction. The books of Kings were written later than Samuel, probably during the exile, although they were based upon earlier sources. In his epoch-making *Beiträge* of 1806–1807 de Wette had cut his teeth, so to speak, on Chronicles, arguing that they were very late books, dependent on Samuel and Kings, and falsely projecting back to the time of David cultic arrangments that had begun to be introduced only in the time of Josiah.[3] This view of Chronicles was substantially repeated in the *Introductions*.

For the remainder of the books of the Old Testament I shall select some pertinent points. Isaiah is divided into First Isaiah (1–39) and Second Isaiah (40–66), but chs. 1–39 contain later material such as chs. 13–14, 24–27 and 34–35. Not all of Jeremiah can be assigned to the prophet, and among the passages that have been added or worked over by a later hand is ch. 31, where occurs the passage about the New Covenant. Ezekiel, on the other hand, is accepted as the work of the prophet of

---

3.   W.M.L. de Wette, *Beiträge zur Einleitung in das Alte Testament* (Halle, 1806–1807).

that name. The Psalms contain many pieces completed shortly before, during and after the Babylonian exile. De Wette rejected the Maccabean dating of some psalms, while remaining sympathetic to the reasons why Maccabean datings had been proposed, on the basis of the content of some of the psalms, for example Psalms 44, 55 and 74.

Old Testament criticism as it had developed in Germany by 1852 was well on the way to becoming what we are familiar with today. It differed from biblical criticism today in degree rather than in kind; and many positions that would be widely accepted today had been established by 1852.

2. How Much did Maurice Know about
Old Testament Criticism as Described Above?

Although Maurice apparently knew some German, he could not read it fluently. In a letter to Miss C. Fox dated 25 February 1848, Maurice wrote 'my knowledge of German is miserably defective'.[4] He thus declined to comment on a translation of something by Schleiermacher she had sent to him. Granted that Maurice was dependent upon works in English, what could he have known about biblical criticism, especially that in German? The obvious starting point must be Hugh James Rose's sermons preached before the University of Cambridge and published in 1825 under the title *The State of the Protestant Religion in Germany*. Maurice went up to Cambridge in 1823, and it is virtually certain that he heard Rose deliver the sermons in question. In an autobiographical letter written in 1831 Maurice stated:

> In the Cambridge pulpit Mr Hugh Rose, afterwards a kind friend of mine denounced German Rationalism, and seemed to treat all German theology as rationialist.[5]

From Rose's sermons and their published version Maurice would have learned that J.S. Vater and W.M.L. de Wette rejected the traditional view that Moses wrote the Pentateuch, and that de Wette and C.P.W. Gramberg had attacked the historical value of the books of Chronicles. Rose also discussed J.P. Gabler's edition of J.G. Eichhorn's *Urgeschichte*. This work, published between 1790 and 1793, offered a

---

4.   Maurice, *The Life of Frederick Denison Maurice*, I, p. 453.
5.   *Life of F.D. Maurice*, I, p. 180.

demythologized interpretation of the opening chapters of Genesis.[6] The story of Adam and Eve was a true story of the first two human beings, but its present form resulted from the simple naivity of the human race and its infancy. Its proper interpretation required the removal of all crude supernatural elements. Thus, the serpent did not speak to Eve. It probably ate some fruit from a particular tree. When Eve and Adam did likewise, they were slightly poisoned by the fruit, and the resulting shock made them aware of their sexual differences and potential. A thunder storm seemed like the voice of a reproving God, and in terror they fled from the garden and could not find their way back to it. This approach, then, would have been familiar to Maurice through Hugh Rose's work.

Eight years after the publication of Hugh Rose's sermons, his younger brother Henry John Rose delivered the Hulsean Lectures in Cambridge under the title *The Law of Moses, Viewed in Connexion with the History and Character of the Jews*. The published version of the lectures (1834) contained an appendix entitled 'The Times at which the Pentateuch and the Historical Books of the Old Testament are Stated, by the Chief Continental Authorities of Recent Celebrity, to have been Written or Compiled'.[7] This gave in tabular form the views on authorship held by W. Gesenius, de Wette, Gramberg and several other scholars. The main part of the book contained one of the very few expositions ever undertaken in English of Gramberg's massive 1200-page *Kritische Geschichte der Religionsideen des Alten Testaments*.[8] Gramberg's book presented a radical version of the history of Israelite religion based partly upon de Wette's researches, in which the notion was rejected that Moses had instituted a fully-fledged system of priesthood and sacrifice. These were much later developments in ancient Israel. In view of Maurice's friendship with Hugh Rose it would be surprising if he was unfamiliar with the work of Henry Rose.

Another work which Maurice could well have read was Samuel Davidson's *Sacred Hermeneutics*, published in 1843.[9] This massive work of over 700 pages included an account of the work of German

---

6. For details see my *Myth in Old Testament Interpretation* (BZAW, 134; Berlin: de Gruyter, 1974), ch. 1.

7. See J.W. Rogerson, *Old Testament Criticism in the Nineteenth Century, England and Germany* (London: SPCK, 1984), pp. 173-75.

8. *Old Testament Criticism*, pp. 57-63, also gives an account of Gramberg's work.

9. See *Old Testament Criticism*, pp. 197-208 for an account of Davidson.

scholars such as Eichhorn, Vater and de Wette. The 'mythical' interpretation of Genesis advocated by Eichhorn and Gabler and previously
mentioned by Hugh Rose was also outlined. New works discussed by
Davidson included two commentaries on Genesis, of which that by Peter
von Bohlen rejected the view that Moses wrote the Pentateuch, and
maintained that many of the narratives in the Pentateuch were
unhistorical. Davidson also pointed out that writers such as de Wette and
Gesenius interpreted Isaiah 52–53 with reference not to Jesus, but to
Israel or to a prophet of ancient Israel. None of the books on Maurice
that I have consulted mentions Samuel Davidson, and we cannot be sure
that Maurice knew his work before 1852. They must surely have had
contact when Davidson came to live in London in 1862.

We know for certain that Maurice read Francis Newman's anony-
mously published *A History of the Hebrew Monarchy* which appeared in
1847.[10] In 1848, as Queen's College was being established, the question
was raised as to whether some of the professors at University College,
London, might be involved in the teaching at Queen's.[11] If the scheme
went forward, one of the teachers involved would be Francis Newman,
who had been appointed Professor of Latin at University College in
1846. In a letter dated 29 April Maurice expressed strong reservations
about allowing Newman to teach at Queen's College. He wrote:

> Those who have attended my lectures on the Scripture know, though the
> last thing I have ever thought of has been to attack Miss Martineau or Mr
> Newman, yet that I have formally, distinctly, consistently, vehemently
> arrived at working out an idea diametrically the opposite of that which is
> set forth in the books on Egypt and the Hebrew monarchy.[12]

The book on Egypt was Harriet Martineau's *Eastern Life, Present and
Past* which, published in 1848, gave an account of Martineau's travels
to Egypt, Sinai, Palestine and Syria in 1847. Among other things it
argued that Moses had got the idea of monotheism from Egyptian
priests. What of Francis Newman on the Hebrew monarchy? It was a
candid account of the difficulties contained in the narratives of the books
of Samuel and Kings. 1 Samuel, with its multiple accounts of Saul's rise
to the kingship, as well as the difficulty that in 1 Samuel 11 Saul defeats
the Ammonites while in 1 Samuel 13 his forces seem to have no

10. See *Old Testament Criticism*, pp. 192-96.
11. Queen's College was a pioneering project in providing higher education for
women. The teachers involved gave their services free of charge.
12. *The Life of F.D. Maurice*, I, p. 470.

weapons and are completely at the mercy of the Philistines, is handled roughly. The books of Chronicles are ridiculed for their inaccuracies and exaggerations. More importantly, Newman argues that the Pentateuch as we know it cannot have existed before the time of Josiah, and that it was only after Josiah's reform that the laws of the Pentateuch began to receive their final shape and public recognition. If Maurice had read only Newman's *The Hebrew Monarchy,* and we know that he had read it, he would have been familiar with much of what was stated or implied in de Wette's *Einleitung* of 1852.

3. *What were Maurice's Critical Views in regard to the Old Testament?*

Most of Maurice's use of the Old Testament, we must remind ourselves, is in sermons; and I would strongly maintain, as a preacher myself, that sermons are not the proper place to discuss or air matters of biblical criticism. It is remarkable, then, that Maurice said as much as he did about historical-critical matters in his sermons, as the examples that I shall now bring illustrate. I begin with Maurice's discussion of whether the book of Isaiah is a unity, a matter that comes up in a sermon preached on 29 March 1852 on Isa. 13.1.[13] Maurice noted the problem that the chapter begins by referring to Babylon. How could this reference to Babylon be understood, since the dominant power of Isaiah's day was not Babylon but Assyria, and Babylon would not threaten Judah for another hundred years or so? Maurice acknowledged the force of the argument for assigning Isaiah 13 and other material to a later prophet:

> Some of the bolder critics of our own time,—finding great difficulties in an interpretation which breaks the harmony of the prophet's visions, and destroys their application to the people among whom he was dwelling and whom he was sent to warn,—have decreed that all these passages, together with all the chapters after the fortieth, must have been written subsequently to the Chaldean captivity, probably in the age of Ezra, and that they have been mixed with the genuine discourses of Isaiah by a compiler.[14]

Although Maurice would reject this view in favour of the traditional acceptance of all 66 chapters as belonging to Isaiah of Jerusalem, he was prepared to allow that the interpolation theory, as he called it, was not necessarily incompatible with faith:

13. *Prophets and Kings*, pp. 273-91.
14. *Prophets and Kings*, p. 280.

the mere sentimental feeling which attaches a particular passage to a particular name will be readily sacrificed by a lover of truth. The more firmly we believe the Bible to be from God, the less serious will that sacrifice seem to us. We shall hear God's voice speaking to us by whatever appellation we denote him who is the instrument of the communication.[15]

There was, therefore, no contradiction for Maurice in accepting the Bible as a divine revelation while at the same time rejecting traditional views about who had written it. If Maurice preferred to side with the traditionalist on this particular issue it was for three reasons. First, he did not wish to depart from the weight of Christian and Jewish tradition without good reason. Secondly, he believed that the researches of the German historian B.G. Niebuhr had shown that although Babylon was part of the Assyrian empire when Isaiah was prophesying, it was nonetheless a powerful city, a city that was 'the seat of the graven images of the gods'. In the 1879 edition of *Prophets and Kings* there is a reference to Niebuhr's *Lectures on Ancient History* to support Maurice's contention.[16] Thirdly, Maurice believed that the reference to Babylon in Isaiah 13 was part of a Babylonian typology running through the Bible, in which Babylon symbolized human attempts to establish a society which owed nothing to God and raised its rulers above all law and obligation.

Maurice, then, even if he did not accept the Second Isaiah theory, was willing to discuss it, and to allow that 'lovers of truth' could accept such positions without being disloyal to the Bible as revelation. This mildly critical stance is also apparent in Maurice's treatment of passages in Isaiah traditionally held to have a reference to Jesus. Maurice preached on Isaiah and Ahaz on 14 March 1852,[17] and in dealing with Isa. 7.14 concentrated on the meaning of the sign in the context of the times of the prophet and the king. Drawing attention to the words 'Before the child shall know to refuse the evil, and choose the good, the land that thou abhorrest shall be forsaken of both her kings', Maurice insisted that this could only mean that a child would be born very soon. To claim otherwise would be 'to set aside the letter of Scripture' utterly. Indeed, Maurice goes on to say: 'There is no warrant at all...for supposing that the birth...was, in the sense we commonly give to the word, miraculous'.[18] Hinting at Christian use of the passage as a prophecy of

15. *Prophets and Kings*, p. 280.
16. *Prophets and Kings*, p. 291.
17. *Prophets and Kings*, pp. 236-54.
18. *Prophets and Kings*, p. 249.

the birth of Jesus, Maurice declared: 'We cannot anticipate an after and more glorious event by supposing the exact parallel of it to have occurred now'.[19]

Maurice argued that any link between Isa. 7.14 and the New Testament should be established by the meaning of the name of the child to be born—Immanuel, God with us—and he illustrated this powerfully. To press for a historical rather than a christological interpretation of Isa. 7.14 was a brave thing to do in Britain in the Church of England in 1852; and Maurice was unrepentant.

> Perhaps you will feel that I have done something to weaken the application of the words which were spoken to Ahaz. By taking them in connection with the falling and raising again of many in Israel in Isaiah's day, I may seem to have denied the truth of St Matthew's sentence 'Now all this was done, that it might be fulfilled which was spoken of the Lord by the prophet: Behold a Virgin shall be with child...' I hope and trust that I have rather been helping you to see the full power and exact truth of that sentence.[20]

However, with Maurice's commitment to a historical reading of passages such as Isa. 7.14 and a readiness to allow that, in principle, there was no objection to something like the Second Isaiah theory, we reach the limits of Maurice's openness to the biblical criticism of his day. On other matters, he was either irritatingly obscure, or candidly against the findings of criticism.

A typical piece of irritating obscurity is his treatment of the book of Jonah, in a sermon dated 25 April 1852.[21] Maurice acknowledged that Jonah was unlike other prophetic books because it was a narrative written in the third person. He also alluded to Jonah's being swallowed by a great fish as 'an event...which has drawn away the minds of readers, especially trivial and superficial readers from the other part of it'. Thus he was not surprised that 'some have fancied it contains a parable instead of a history'.

For his part, Maurice could find no pretext for the notion that the book of Jonah does not describe processes in the heart of a real man, and maintained that nothing in the narrative suggested that it was written by a sophist using an old name to conceal a composition of his own. This being so, what does Maurice make of the great fish that swallows Jonah? To this I can only reply: I do not know. Maurice's narrative

19. *Prophets and Kings*, p. 249.
20. *Prophets and Kings*, p. 252.
21. *Prophets and Kings*, pp. 351-69.

about the great fish incident is as follows: 'In the jaws of desolation and death, he cries to God, confesses his sin, submits to his punishment. He is delivered, and goes forth once more on his errand.'[22] Elsewhere in the sermon, Maurice obfuscates as follows:

> One who considers how great and wonderful a thing a preservation from the deep is, who believes that the Lord is the author of every such preservation, who feels at the same time that he does not understand, and is never likely to understand the method of this particular preservation, dwells on that which must at all events be the essence of the story, and leaves its incidents as he finds them.[23]

This is the Maurice of the interpretation of Baalam's talking ass, who is content to accept that the ass made noises that conveyed a message to its owner. Where he cannot accept the findings of biblical criticism, Maurice is candid, and even sarcastic. Discussing the narratives of Genesis he declares:

> Readers are sure when they lay down the book of Genesis that they have perused a very marvellous narrative. Learned critics supply them with a phrase, and tell them that they have not been occupied with history in the strict sense, but with mythical stories which contain moral or spiritual lessons of more or less value. Alas for men who spend all their lives in their studies, and have never yet discovered that birth, marriage, death, burial, belong to the facts, and not to the legends, of mankind![24]

Again, Maurice gave short shrift to the idea that there were two sources in 1 Samuel because of the duplication of incidents: 'It is the fashion of our times to suppose that there must be two versions of the same fact preserved by different chroniclers, and brought together by some careless compiler'. Maurice's solution was the belief that there occur in most of our lives events, often separated by many years, which look as if one was the repetition of the other.[25]

We can summarize Maurice's other views by saying that he accepted Moses as the author of the Pentateuch, including Deuteronomy, and David as the author of many psalms. Commenting on the story of the discovery of the book of the law in the temple in 622 BCE, he contented himself with the observation that 'the book of the law of the Lord, it seems, had become a strange and unknown book even to Shaphan the

22. *Prophets and Kings*, p. 356.
23. *Prophets and Kings*, p. 353.
24. *Patriarchs and Lawgivers*, p. 103.
25. *Prophets and Kings*, p.18.

scribe and Hilkiah the priest'.[26] This is much less fun than Francis Newman's discussion of the implications of the discovery of the law book![27]

In regard to biblical criticism, Maurice was a transitional figure in nineteenth-century Britain, and all the more important for being so. He interpreted the Old Testament in its historical setting, and not as a set of prophecies about Jesus. He allowed that challenging traditional views of authorship of Old Testament books was not a challenge to the integrity of the Old Testament. He allowed the right of criticism and did not cry 'rationalist' or 'unbeliever' when considering critical views. If he did not accept many critical views it was mainly beause he felt that their advocates did not know enough about real life. The limits of openness are indicated by his attitude to *Essays and Reviews* and Part I of Colenso's *The Pentateuch and Joshua*.

4. *Reactions to* Essays and Reviews *and* The Pentateuch and Joshua

On the face of it, there was nothing in *Essays and Reviews*, seven essays by members of the Church of England which appeared in 1860, to which Maurice could or should have taken exception.[28] Frederick Temple's essay on 'The Education of the World' addressed one of Maurice's favourite themes, education, offered a traditional reading of the history of Israelite religion, minimized the doctrine of the Fall, and saw educative value in God's punishments of Israel's frequent acts of disobedience. Roland Williams's elusive essay on Bunsen, again, could hardly cause offence to Maurice. Maurice had met Bunsen, admired Bunsen's mentor Niebuhr, and must surely have applauded Bunsen's attempt to use ancient history in general to vindicate the broad outline of Old Testament history. With C.W. Goodwin's essay on Genesis 1–3

26. *Prophets and Kings*, p. 378.
27. Newman argued that if the law had been published before the time of Josiah, it was difficult to explain how and when things had reached such a condition that a reform was needed. Further, if the law had existed and Josiah 'upheld the rites of Baal and Moloch, and left a graven image of Astare in Jehovah's house, and, while acquainted with Leviticus repented not; neither would he have repented when Deuteronomy rose from the dead'. All this indicated that the law had not been published before Josiah's time. See F. Newman, *A History of the Hebrew Monarchy from the Administration of Samuel to the Babylonian Captivity* (London, 1847), p. 335.
28. See *Old Testament Criticism*, pp. 209-19.

Maurice might well have been unhappy. This essayist described these chapters as instances of the scientific outlook of the time when the narrative was written. Maurice's interpretation was much more symbolic. Jowett's essay on the interpretation of Scripture contains much that Maurice must surely have endorsed. Interpretation must begin with the historical circumstances of the writers of the Old Testament before the interpreter sees the whole as part of a progressive unfolding of the character of God, reaching its climax in Jesus Christ.

Maurice's reactions to *Essays and Reviews* were set out in letters written in the first part of 1861. To A.P. Stanley he wrote:

> As my only hope of resisting the devil worship of the religious world lies in preaching the full revelation of God in Christ set forth in the Bible, I cannot have much sympathy with the book generally.[29]

Maurice went on to say, however, that what he called 'the orthodoxy which covers our Atheism' needed to be broken down by books such as *Essays and Reviews*. In another letter Maurice stated that the deficiencies of the writers of the essays were more serious than their utterances, and a further comment was:

> I should say of every one [of the essayists] 'The writer does not *mean* to be negative, does not *mean* to overthrow the faith. He is confused by what he sees around him and feels within him.[30]

My own view of what distressed Maurice about *Essays and Reviews* is the following. In the essays by Temple and Jowett, and to a lesser extent that by Goodwin, the idea of progressive education is used in such a way that the Hebrews of the Old Testament are treated as primitives whose views can only be evidence for an inferior religion now superseded. Temple wrote of the Mosaic system:

> There is very little directly spiritual. No freedom of conduct or opinion is allowed...The teaching of the Law was followed by the comments of the Prophets. It is impossible to mistake the complete change of tone and spirit.[31]

Maurice, who held that in every part of the Old Testament there was a record of God dealing with humankind, a record meant for the illumination of readers, could not have agreed with these sentiments. The

---

29. *Life of F.D. Maurice*, II, pp. 382-83.
30. *Life of F.D. Maurice*, II, pp. 389-90.
31. F. Temple, 'The Education of the World', in *Essays and Reviews* (London, 5th edn, 1861), p. 8.

essayists seemed to be saying that the Bible was information about a historical process of the divine education of humanity. Maurice did not quite see it like that. For him, the Bible revealed not an educating process, but an educating God; and even if that educating God was dealing with Moses and the people of the exodus, he was doing it in a way that made the record of this dealing a word of God for contemporary readers.

Maurice's reactions to Colenso's *The Pentateuch and Joshua* are more readily understandable.[32] The two men had known each other for many years, Colenso had been impressed by *The Kingdom of Christ*, and Maurice had officiated at Colenso's marriage in 1846. In 1856, by which time Colenso was a missionary bishop working among the Zulu in Natal, Maurice wrote to Mrs Colenso:

> Do tell the bishop, with my kindest love, that the battle he is fighting is ours also; nothing less than whether the devil or the Father of our Lord Jesus Christ is the God.[33]

For his part, Colenso dedicated a volume of sermons to Maurice in October 1852, at a time when Maurice was under fierce attack on account of his *Theological Essays*.[34]

Part I of the *Pentateuch and Joshua*, which appeared in 1862, was a devastating attack on the historical credibility of the narrative of the exodus and wilderness wanderings. Beginning from the statement at Exod. 12.37 that 600,000 males aged twenty and upwards left Egypt, Colenso estimated that over two million Hebrews must have taken part in the exodus, plus two million sheep, and 50,000 oxen required to carry the 200,000 tents in which they would have lived. This column, crossing the Red Sea, would have been enormously long, because even the 600,000 marching five abreast, and with a yard between each rank, would have stretched out to a distance of 68 miles. At the Passover, the three priests (there were only Aaron, Eleazer and Ithamar) would have sacrificed the lambs at a rate of 1000 per minute. The Israelites, encamped, would have formed a square twelve miles by twelve miles, a fact that would have meant a long journey for those living near the centre to attend to the calls of nature. Deut. 23.12 commands that calls of nature have to be relieved 'outside the camp'.

32. See *Old Testament Criticism*, pp. 220-37.
33. *Life of F.D. Maurice*, II, p. 296.
34. *Life of F.D. Maurice*, II, p. 185.

Colenso was almost universally condemned by the church and other circles in Britain; yet the fact that there was substance to his criticisms was borne out from a very unlikely source some years later. When the Roman Catholic scholar M.-J. Lagrange visited Sinai in 1893 and realized that the area could not possibly have supported the number of Israelites mentioned in Exodus and Numbers, he became convinced of the value of the documentary theory that assigned these narratives to the late Priestly source.[35]

Be that as it may, Maurice was devastated by 'the most purely negative criticism I ever read',[36] had a painful meeting with his erstwhile friend following some fruitless correspondence, and felt that it was Colenso's clear duty to resign his bishopric. Three years after the publication of Part I of the *The Pentateuch and Joshua* Maurice wrote to a clergyman in South Africa:

> When [Colenso] set himself at war with the Jewish economy and the life of the Old Testament I was utterly struck down. I had always believed that the great barrier against ecclesiastical oppression and tyranny, the great hold upon the conscience of the English nation, the great hope of every nation, lay in asserting the maxim that God is Himself the Deliverer, that His name is the ground of national liberty. To have a quantity of criticism about the dung in the Jewish camp, and the division of a hare's foot, thrown in my face, when I was satisfied that the Jewish history had been the mightiest witness to the people for a living God against the dead dogmas of priests, was more shocking to me than I can describe...I must have seemed very cold and cruel to Colenso; often I seemed so to myself. But the duty of vindicating the Old Testament as the great witness for liberty appeared to me a paramount one.[37]

One of the tragedies of the split between the two men was that, in some ways, they were not as far apart as it may seem. Colenso was as opposed to ecclesiastical bondage as Maurice, and saw in biblical criticism a way of de-emphasizing the priestly and levitical parts of the Old Testament by showing them to be late developments. As to his achievements, A.P. Stanley said in a speech to the Society for the Propagation of the Gospel:

---

35. M.-J. Lagrange, *Personal Reflections and Memoirs* (New York: Paulist Press, 1985), pp. 38-40.

36. *Life of F.D. Maurice*, II, p. 427.

37. *Life of F.D. Maurice*, II, p. 490.

The Bishop of Natal is the one colonial bishop who has translated the Bible into the languages of the natives of his diocese. He is the one colonial bishop who, when he believed a native to be wronged, left his diocese, journeyed to London, and never rested till he had procured the reversal of that wrong. He is the one colonial bishop who, as soon as he had done this, returned immediately to his diocese and his work. For these acts he has never received any praise, any encouragement, from this, the oldest of our missionary societies.[38]

Subsequent biblical criticism has supported Colenso's admittedly intemperate criticism against Maurice's conservatism. But is it possible that, in his opposition to what he regarded as forms of criticism that drew attention away from the central message of the Old Testament, Maurice had seen something that others missed, something that we need to see today?

In my final lecture I shall ask if Maurice has anything to teach us about the interpretation of the Old Testament in our day and to our world.

38. R.E. Prothero and G.G. Bradley, *The Life and Correspondence of Arthur Penrhyn Stanley DD, Late Dean of Westminster* (London, 1893), II, p. 295.

Chapter 3

MAURICE AND BIBLICAL STUDIES TODAY

Maurice was deeply upset by the Old Testament criticism of his day, as we find it in Colenso and, to a lesser extent, the contributors to *Essays and Reviews*. As we saw in the second lecture, Maurice was not opposed in principle to historical criticism. He was also prepared to allow that there were errors in the biblical record. His biographer son states Maurice's opinion 'that the mistakes, however numerous, did not affect [the] historical reality and veracity' of the book of Exodus.[1] What seems to have distressed Maurice most was the attitude to the Bible that biblical criticism seemed to engender. Colenso appeared to *enjoy* finding absurdities in the text; seemed to *enjoy* refuting defenders of the accuracy of the biblical records; seemed to enjoy the esteem in which scholars on the continent began to hold him. Maurice could not reconcile this with his belief that the Old Testament was in some sense the authentic record of God's dealings with a real people and real individuals among that people; and let me add for the sake of ensuring that no one leaves this lecture thinking that I have a poor estimate of Colenso, that I have as great a regard for him as I have for Maurice and can sympathize fully with Colenso's exasperation with his critics.

Where does this leave us? Is it the end of the story? Are we to regard Maurice as essentially a pre-critical scholar, for all his alleged openness to historical criticism? Is he separated from us by a barrier that we can cross in historical imagination, but which then leaves us stranded in a world that is quite different from our own? In this final lecture I propose to look at Maurice's Old Testament work in the light of the new concerns that have emerged in the past twenty years: literary readings of the Old Testment, liberation readings and feminist readings. I shall consider whether these recent approaches offer resources which, if they had been available to Maurice, would have helped him to be more accommodating

1.   *Life of F.D. Maurice*, II, p. 449.

to biblical criticism without compromising what he believed to be the main purpose of the Bible.

Inevitably, what I shall do will involve speculation, and the result will be strongly slanted in favour of my own particular interests. But in this post-modern age, readings, or re-readings, of the work of past scholars have shed light on their work, and have played a part in helping modern issues to be explored and addressed. It is in this spirit that I approach my task.

I begin with literary readings of the Bible. Maurice believed that the narratives about the characters in the book of Genesis were narratives about real people. Adam and Eve are the couple from which the human race descended; the great ages of those who lived before the Flood, in some cases over 900 years, are puzzling but accepted: 'I have always heard that they came to be rather old gentlemen, and not having any reason to disbelieve it, I supposed they were';[2] and there was no doubt about the existence of the patriarchs from Abraham onwards. There would seem to be no point of contact between this position and a modern conservatively-critical belief that even if Abraham existed, the stories about him have been so shaped in transmission that he has become a type, and has been robbed of his historical identity.

It is here, we might suppose, that modern literary readings of the Bible could come to Maurice's aid; for such readings do not ask whether Eve or Abraham existed. They ask how Eve and Abraham function as characters in a narrative. The meaning of the narratives is not sought in the form of information about the historical Eve or Abraham. The narrative suggests or conveys meaning through the interplay of plot, dialogue, characters, role and so on.

The work in which we might expect to find Maurice exploring the dimensions and portrayal of Old Testament characters is *The Prophets and Kings of the Old Testament*; but we are disappointed if we look for anything here that we could see in terms of a modern literary reading. Maurice rarely deals with the complete portrayal of an Old Testament person. Rather, he fastens onto particular incidents, and uses them as opportunities to enlarge on general moral or theological topics. The closest he comes to a literary reading is in his sermon on Jonah and Nahum, preached on 25 April 1852.[3]

In the second lecture I touched on Maurice's far from satisfactory treatment of the historicity of Jonah, and of the big fish incident. In this

2. *Life of F.D. Maurice*, I, p. 311.
3. *Prophets and Kings*, pp. 351-69.

lecture I shall be more positive about the treatment of the book of Jonah. In his discussion of its historicity Maurice allows, in a passage of great importance to which I shall return later, that a narrative which expresses the reflections of an author upon past traditions can be as important as a 'straight' narrative about what happened to a historical person. Or, to put it another way, Maurice accepted that writers who are trying 'to understand the principles of God's government' can present their convictions by reinterpreting traditions about past events. Thus Maurice does not completely reject the idea that the book of Jonah might be a kind of inspired fiction based upon a story about a venerable seer. Maurice is aware of the literary and dramatic aspects of the book of Jonah; and he links this acknowledgment of its literary powers to his belief that it was a *real* history by saying that 'a man should be an artist to write a biography as much as to write a romance'.[4]

In his treatment of Jonah, Maurice offers some brilliant pasages which do full justice to the many ironies that the book contains. Here is a notable example:

> [Jonah] is a new man; he who was lately shut up in death, can speak of God's truth and righteousness. [But] though he has experienced much mercy, he is not told to proclaim mercy. He is told to cry aloud in all the streets of the great Nineveh, that sin has been committed and that sin must bring death. He has been used to utter such sounds in Samaria and they have fallen utterly dead. No one has thought them worth listening to. Unspeakable marvel! Here, instead of being dead words, they seen able to waken the dead...The Message has done its work. God has triumphed. But Jonah has not triumphed. He is utterly confounded and sick at heart; he has deceived others and deceived himself. He had expected to see men, women, children, cattle, all perishing; but they all lived. He had expected—, had he hoped it?[5]

This quotation shows that Maurice would have excelled if he had worked at a time when literary readings of biblical texts were in vogue. But I venture to think that he would have been unhappy about the implication of literary readings. While they would rescue him from the question of whether Eve and Abraham were real people, they would exact a price that Maurice would not have been prepared to pay.

Literary readings of the Bible that want to suggest that there is more to this approach than mere entertainment often talk about the world of

4.   *Prophets and Kings*, p. 354.
5.   *Prophets and Kings*, pp. 358-59.

the text. This world may have different values from our world, or may perceive reality in a different way from us. Being immersed in the 'world of the text', we are told, changes and challenges us, and we come back to our own world as different people. My colleague David Clines has expressed this view as follows:

> What is offered in a story is a 'world'—make-believe or real, familiar or unfamiliar. To the degree that the hearer or reader of the story is imaginatively seized by the story, to that degree he or she 'enters' the world of the story. That means that the reader of the story, when powerfully affected by it, becomes a participant of its world.[6] The Pentateuch becomes such a source of life...through the reader's patient engagement with the text and openness to being seized, challenged, or threatened by the 'world' it lays bare.[7]

Maurice would, I think, have been unhappy about the idea of a world of a story or text possibly different from our own. He is forever insisting that the world of the Bible is *our* world, that prophets are not different in kind from other people, including ourselves, that religion is not a specialized compartment but a window on the whole of reality. Maurice insists that because the Bible is the record of God at work in *our* world, it must be considered with the greatest possible seriousness. This leaves us with the dilemma from which we began, that Maurice believed that Eve and Abraham were real people, whereas we say, at best, that Abraham may have existed but we have no real information about him, only stories shaped in order to express certain themes. I shall try another way of facing this dilemma a little later; but next, I shall consider what Maurice might have made of liberation readings of the Old Testament.

It is, of course, a mistake to think that there is one single approach that can be called liberation theology. When it comes to the Old Testament, liberation approaches can range from Norman Gottwald's attempt to reconstruct and to privilege an egalitarian society in the period before the rise of the monarchy in Israel to Itumelong J. Mosala's contention that the Old Testament is partly flawed because it originated from the class of oppressors. However, all those who read the Old Testament from a liberation perspective would presumably agree that the aim of such reading is to bring about liberation in practice. How would Maurice have felt about this?

6.   D.J.A. Clines, *The Theme of the Pentateuch* (JSOTSup, 10; Sheffield: JSOT Press, 1979), p. 102.

7.   *Theme of the Pentateuch*, p. 118.

It is beyond my competence to give an account of Maurice's practical work for what might generally be called 'liberation' in the society of his day. Alec Vidler described Maurice as a man of thought rather than a man of action, made more for uttering prophecies than for framing policies.[8] But he adds that Maurice 'was always eager to move out in to action' and he quotes Maurice to the effect that the test of all principles affecting to be moral and human must be their application to the circumstances in which we are placed.

Two small illustrations will serve to show how Maurice was active in movements for social improvement. As part of his involvement with the associations for co-operative production, Maurice and his wife made themselve responsible for renting 31 Red Lion Square so that they could help found the North London Needlewomen's Association. This co-operative provided lodgings and employment for over twenty dress-makers and milliners, paid them a small allowance and ensured their employment when orders were slack.[9]

The second illustration concerns Maurice's attitude to the engineering and iron trades strike and lock-out early in 1852. This bitter dispute, reminiscent of the miners' strike in Britain in the late 1980s in that a powerful employer forced the workers to capitulate gradually, brought great anguish to Maurice. His approach was original and his sympathy genuine, as an extract from one of his letters shows. Answering the accusation that he had urged the striking workers to surrender he realized that

> what I said to the council was that I believed an unconditional surrender might be the right way of showing the brute force there was in capital, and of bringing the case of the working-men fairly before the public, as a struggle of human beings against mere money power. But I will not ask the men to starve, unless I can starve with them...I will not deceive them by false promises and hopes, and call upon them for sacrifices, which they may not be morally or physically able to make...I did not suppose the iron workers could be induced, or ought to be induced...to surrender; but I did think, that that alternative might be set before them...not as an escape from what is right, but as a way of enforcing it.[10]

8. A.R. Vidler, *F.D. Maurice and Company: Nineteenth-Century Studies* (London: SCM Press, 1966), p. 177.

9. C.E. Raven, *Christian Socialism, 1848–1854* (London: Macmillan, 1920), p. 210.

10. *Life of F.D. Maurice*, II, p. 107.

It so happens that, as the lock-out began on 10 January 1852, Maurice was preparing a sermon on the revolt of Jeroboam after the death of Solomon, a sermon which he preached on 18 January. It is a striking and original piece. Maurice traced the antecedents of the division of the kingdom back to Solomon's idolatry, by which he did not mean Solomon's worship of other gods, but his love of material things and human achievements for their own sake. Such idolatry was a denial of God's rule; and disaster followed as inevitably as if natural laws regarding the sea or fire had been ignored. But moral laws needed human agents to defend them; and in the case of the division of the kingdom the human agent used by God was Jeroboam. This was in spite of the repeated assertion in the books of Kings that Jeroboam did evil and caused Israel to sin. Indeed, Maurice's account of Jeroboam's work arising out of the prophecy of Ahijah is almost complimentary:

> [Jeroboam] is…acquainted with the discontents of the people; apparently, he sympathises with them. It is not said or even hinted that he felt the horror which Ahijah felt of Solomon's superstition…He appears as the spokesman and representative of those who were oppressed by Solomon's exactions for building Millo and repairing the breaches in the city of David. The tyranny grew out of the idolatry. Though Jeroboam might not perceive the root, he could perceive the evil fruit, which deserved to be hated for its own sake; he was therefore qualified to execute Ahijah's prophecy, not merely as a dull instrument, but as one who had, to a certain extent, a righteous purpose.[11]

Thus we find Maurice preaching during a time of national emergency, and declaring that a man who led a revolt on behalf of oppressed people had a righteous purpose, and was a worthy instrument to carry out the defence of injustice resulting from idolatry. Commenting on the advice of the young men who urged Rehoboam to make the burdens of the people heavier, Maurice made a veiled reference to the industrial turmoil of his day.

> How rapidly the interval of 3,000 years,—how all the difference between a small Syrian province of the old world, and a nation of Europe in the nineteenth century, seems to disappear, as we read this story!…'I will chastise you with scorpions'—this in all ages has been the childish bluster of men who have made themselves blind to the future by refusing to use their eyes in judging of that which is before them;—who fancy that the

11. *Prophets and Kings*, pp. 95-96.

power will be their own for ever at the very moment when the handwriting
on the wall is declaring that it has been taken from them and given to
another.[12]

Maurice did not himself advocate or necessarily condone resistance by
oppressed workers again their employers. In the case of Jeroboam, he
was commenting on a narrative of events that had taken place, and he
was using them to point out what he regarded as the root cause of
them—namely, idolatry, or the disregard of God and the pursuit of
power and wealth for their own sake. When he criticized Jeroboam later
in his sermon it was because Jeroboam tried to consolidate his kingdom
by setting up human forms of security rather than by seeking God's
will. In his attitude to the iron trades lock-out of 1852 Maurice did not
condemn the leaders, but suggested an unsuual solution, namely,
surrender, designed to unmask the idolatry that he undoubtedly believed
was at the root of the attitude of the employers. I think that we can be
sure that Maurice would have endorsed certain types of liberation
readings of the Old Testament, and that he might have had distinctive
views to add to them. Certainly, I want to think further about Maurice's
possible contribution to liberation readings of the Bible.

While we are considering liberation readings of the Old Testament, it
is worth pausing to ask about feminist readings. Maurice was, after all, a
pioneer in women's education. Does he deal sympathetically with
women in the Old Testament? The answer is no; but it is an interesting
no. The titles of his books of Old Testament sermons, *Patriarchs and
Lawgivers* and *Prophets and Kings*, do not encourage us to expect
much about women, and the outcome is not surprising. Leaving aside
the sermon on Hosea's unfaithful wife, which is hardly good raw material for a sympathetic reading, Maurice's only treatment of women in
the Old Testament is in a sermon delivered on Trinity II, St Peter's Day,
29 June 1851. The set lessons were Judges 4 and 5, and Maurice took as
his text the opening words of the Song of Deborah.

In fact, the main bulk of the sermon is addressed to the problem of
the behaviour of Jael, who had delivered Israel by tricking Sisera, the
commander of the Canaanite armies into her tent, and smashing his head
with a mallet.

'The moral law', Maurice declared, 'recognised in an Arab tent' condemns an act of this kind; and later in the sermon Maurice surmises that

12. *Prophets and Kings*, pp. 97-98.

if Deborah, while exercising the office of a judge, had been asked to adjudicate on the deed that Jael carried out she would have been led—'by her reverence for the law of God and by His teaching,—to inflict the most summary and decisive judgements upon such [an act]'.[13]

In that case, why did Deborah so warmly praise the actions of Jael?

> I am sure that a woman inspired with an intense sense of her country's miseries and wrongs, burning with a desire for the destruction of the oppressor, certain that when he fell he would fall by God's righteous judgments, and not by any achievement of hers or Barak's...I am sure that such a woman could not appreciate the merit or demerit of the instrument who had wrought deliverance for Israel...That at such a moment, any person,—a woman especially,—should lose all other feelings in one indiscriminate emotion of rapture,—should treat all persons who had helped to produce it as worthy of admiration and benediction,—we should all think exceedingly natural.[14]

As I read Maurice here, the view of Deborah and Jael is not flattering. Jael is guilty of what Maurice called 'detestable treachery' while Deborah, although acting exceedingly naturally in praising Jael, is carried away by emotional deelings—feelings most likely to sway the better judgment of a woman in particular. There is, however, one juicy comment in this sermon that is worth quoting. Maurice condemns those who excuse Jael on the grounds that she received a sudden intimation from heaven of the duty to commit the murder. Maurice's reply is devastating:

> We cannot feel comfortable while we believe that the thought of an act which we feel to be treacherous arose in the mind of the wife of Heber the Kenite; we are quite happy if we can believe that it arose in the Divine Mind! I know that when the interpretation presents itself in this form it will make us all shudder. I desire that it should. A number of such blasphemous notions dwell within us in a confused twilight. They must be brought into the clear open day that we may see what they are.[15]

I am sure that we shall all agreee with that !

It is now time to look to other resources that may help us to appreciate Maurice's Old Testament work for our own time. In a recently-published volume of essays, *Deutsche Alttestamentler in drei Jahrhunderten*, Rudolf Smend has reminded us of the distinction that Gerhard von Rad made in his *Theologie des Alten Testaments* between two 'pictures of

13. *Patriarchs and Lawgivers*, p. 334.
14. *Patriarchs and Lawgivers*, p. 332.
15. *Patriarchs and Lawgivers*, p. 331.

the history of Israel'—that of modern historical criticism and that presented by the faith of Israel. The latter, Israel's history as presented by the faith of Israel, was alone the subject of an Old Testament theology.[16] Von Rad himself pointed out that it was impossible to reconcile the picture of Israel's history and religion as reconstructed by modern critical scholarship with the picture of these things as maintained in the Old Testament.

Historical-critical scholarship holds that it is impossible that all Israel was at Sinai, that Israel passed through the Red Sea *en bloc* and invaded the promised land *en bloc*. It also considers that the traditions in the book of Exodus about Moses and his leadership role are as unhistorical as are the roles ascribed to the Judges by the deuteronomistic book of Judges.[17] Von Rad may have been slightly over-sceptical at one or two points here, but we can accept his verdict, because it confronts us with the problem that devastated Maurice when he read Colenso. Maurice accepted the book of Exodus as basically true history even if it contained minor errors of fact; Colenso showed that it could not be regarded as serious history.

Von Rad's solution to the dilemma was to maintain that Israel's own account of its history was a datum; this account existed and as such was of theological significance. An important part of this position was the notion of *Nacherzählung* or re-telling. The Old Testament is not simply an Israelite version of actual events viewed from the perspective of faith, as though the reporters witnessed events and described them in their own, faith-oriented way. The Old Testament contains the re-telling (*Nacherzählung*) of events, the accounts of which had been shaped in many cases by liturgical celebration and recital. Thus, there were many links in the chain from the final form of re-telling to the events that were being recounted, and this was one reason why a modern critical version of the events differed from the Old Testament's version. Further, it was necessary to remember the diversity of Old Testament traditions, and the fact that the prophetic and wisdom strands of the Old Testament related in different ways to the great blocks of retold saving history in the Old Testament.

Von Rad's position sparked off a long and interesting debate in the

16. R. Smend, *Deutsche Alttestamentler in drei Jahrhunderten* (Göttingen: Vandenhoeck & Ruprecht, 1989), p. 48.

17. G. von Rad, *Theologie des Alten Testaments. I. Die Theologie der geschichtlichen Traditionen* (Munich: Chr. Kaiser Verlag, 1961), p. 419.

1960s among Old Testament scholars, of which only some salient points can be noted in this lecture. Some of von Rad's critics accused him of accepting as the word of God a pious lie; and they insisted that if God revealed himself in acts in history, then it was the job of historical-critical scholarship to study these revelatory events, and to make them the basis of theological reflection. Walther Eichrodt posed the question: if a witness to faith has no secure connection to historical reality, can it count as a testimony to historical revelation?[18] On the conservative side, scholars insisted that von Rad's historical scepticism was too extreme, and that historical-critical study had not disproved the saving events that the Old Testament claims as the basis of its existence as the people of God.

Rolf Rendtorff adopted a position that can be described as a refinement of that of von Rad. Basically he regarded von Rad's opposition of historical-critical reconstruction of events to the facts as confessed in the Old Testament by Israel's faith as a false opposition. He pointed out that there are no facts without tradition, and that a tradition of faith about God's acts is itself history. The historical significance of an event often consists in how an event affected those who were involved, and how these effects helped people to define and interpret their existence and identity. Thus, in the Old Testament, encounter with God does not take place in isolated events; it is continually mediated by narratives which proclaim what God has done, so that Israel can trust that he is still at work.[19]

This, it seems to me, brings us close to Maurice. We cannot say where he would have positioned himself had he taken part in the debate sparked off by von Rad. But if we go back to the Jonah sermon, we find something that allowed that *Nacherzählung*, re-telling, could give a true account of God at work even if the re-telling produced a version that would not be entirely accepted by historical-critical reconstruction. The passage reads as follows:

> [The critic] pores over the whale, he forgets God. To the mere critic the appearance of such a prodigy is decisive as to the character of the whole story. It must be merely composed, he concludes, for the sake of a moral;

18. W. Eichrodt, *Old Testament Theology* (London: SCM Press, 1962), I, p. 514. Eichrodt's comments are in an Excursus on von Rad's position.

19. R. Rendtorff, 'Geschichte und Überlieferung', in *Gesammelte Studien zum Alten Testament* (Theologische Bücherei, Altes Testament, 57; Munich: Chr. Kaiser Verlag, 1975), pp. 25-38.

it either is not meant to describe what actually occurred, or the narrator was deceived by a loose tradition of it which had come down from a distant age.[20]

So far Maurice has summed up the problem posed by von Rad admirably. He continues:

> Now, assuredly, if a holy man of some later time were led to meditate upon a story which had been preserved respecting some venerable seer, and to put it forth for the benefit of his contemporaries there is no doubt that the truth which he saw in it would be more important in his eyes than the man who was the subject of it...He would not have been a holy or inspired man if he had not cared more to understand the principles of God's government, and to make them known, than to hear or tell any new thing.[21]

Even allowing for the obscurities of Maurice's style, it seems to me to be quite clear that Maurice is allowing for the following possibility: that a writer who was concerned to understand the principles of God's government could meditate upon an old story, and re-present it. In re-presenting it, this writer would be less concerned with what had originally happened than with bringing out the truths about God's government that he saw in the story. Further, this writer would be inspired and trustworthy, in the sense that his concern for the things of God would help and guide him to see and to say things that were true about God's government.

With this statement I do not imagine that we have completely solved the problem of the lack of fit betwen the Old Testament's understanding of Israel's history and a modern historical-critical reconstruction; but we have gone far enough, in my view, to be able to accommodate Maurice within the parameters of current Old Testament scholarship. Translating Maurice into modern idom, we can say that the Old Testament is a record of belief within ancient Israel of God's encounter with Israel. In that record of belief in God's dealings with his people, God's character is revealed so that readers of the record are challenged to decide for or against the truth of that belief. An acceptance that the record was true would involve more than intellectual assent; it would challenge the person involved to believe that the world is truly ruled by God as claimed in the Bible, and that just as belief in an actual redemption from slavery was the basis of Israel's existence, so belief in an actual

20. *Prophets and Kings*, p. 353.
21. *Prophets and Kings*, p. 353-54.

redemption of all humanity must govern and shape the life and commitments of Christians today.

I hope that Maurice would have endorsed this attempt to modernize him; but whether or not he would have endorsed it, I believe that it frees us up to go back to Maurice's sermons on the Old Testament and to look for things of permanent value.

For myself, I would want to emphasize three points above all others. First, the problems of our world stem from the fact that we do not know how to answer the question 'what does it mean to be human?' For Maurice, this failure was bound up with the attempt of humankind to define humanity in terms of human power, human self-will and human greed. The opposite of this attitude was sacrifice: the making of things new by the surrender of self-will, with all the dangers that this involved. I am reminded again of Maurice's advice to the locked-out iron workers in 1852 to surrender, in the hope that such action would rob the employers of victory and would convict the conscience of the nation in favour of the plight of the workers. It would be a sacrifice that made things new.

Secondly, the reason why Maurice disliked the biblical criticism of his day was because it turned the Bible into an object, an object that was in an inferior position to the critic. He feared that this attitude would make it impossible for people to see the Bible for what it really was: an account of God's dealings with ordinary human beings in the past, so that readers in the present would encounter the same God for themselves. What distressed him when he met Colenso in 1862 was that Colenso seemed to Maurice to have become proud of his achievements as a critic, and to be enjoying the acclaim that he was receiving from some scholars on the continent of Europe. In my view, Maurice has something to teach us here.

It is not my view that Old Testament scholars must either be believers or must leave biblical scholarship to those who are. After all, I work, gladly, in an institution whose statutes make it illegal to apply any religious tests to teachers or students; and I should add that it was events such as the dismissal of Maurice from King's on theological grounds that made institutions such as Sheffield ensure, by statute, that such goings on would not be possible in their academies! But whether we are believers or not, we have to face Maurice's implied question: does our criticism of the Bible turn it into an object for which we have no reverence; or will we at least accord it the status, even as we criticize it, of a stranger who on fuller acquaintance will mutually enrich us?[22]

The third point is an extension of the second. Maurice time and again warns against things becoming ends in themselves, rather than means. He condemns priests who see their office as a set of privileges to be defended against intruders. He condemns churches that put the safeguarding of their power and existence at the top of their agenda. He proclaims that priesthood, churches and religion exist to point to something else—the hallowing of all humanity and all the activities of humanity. He would have said the same about the Bible. Its study is not an end in itself; it is there to enrich and to enable humanity. We can each interpret that for ourselves depending on who we are and to what we are committed. But it is a challenge we should not ignore, and one that we owe it to Maurice to face honestly and sincerely.

22. This analogy is taken from G. Steiner's *Real Presences: Is there Anything* in *What We Say?* (London: Faber & Faber, 1987), pp. 175-76.

Part II

FAITH AND CRITICISM IN THE WORK OF
WILLIAM ROBERTSON SMITH: GIFFORD LECTURES 1994

Chapter 4

A TALE OF TWO CULTURES

On 1 June 1877 the Revd Alex McCraw of Kilbogie wrote to *The Scotsman* to inform its readers that he proposed to bring forward an overture to the next meeting of his Synod. The overture read as follows:

> Whereas a knowledge of the Hebrew language is not necessary to salvation, or the understanding of Divine truth, and whereas it hath in many instances led to the adoption of dangerous and unsound views with regard to the authority of the Word of God, it is humbly overtured to the Venerable Assembly that the teaching of Hebrew, and particularly Biblical Criticism, should henceforth be discontinued in our Colleges, and that all those at present employed in teaching these branches should, from and after the passing of this overture into an Act of the said Venerable Assembly, be relieved from their respective offices, with such regard to their true interests as may seem just.[1]

The timing of the letter was significant, for three days earlier, on 29 May 1877, the General Assembly had voted by a majority of 378 in favour of a motion that William Robertson Smith should be suspended from his post at the Free Church College while the Aberdeen Presbytery considered further the implications of his article 'Bible' in the *Encyclopaedia Britannica*.[2] McCraw, who was a supporter of one of Smith's most implacable opponents, Dr James Begg, was clearly trying to influence the outcome of the forthcoming debate; but this first lecture is not going to be a discussion of Smith's trial, but an attempt to look in a new way at the implications of the trial.

McCraw is important to us in that he was expressing in perhaps an extreme way what many were thinking in the Free Church in 1877. He went on in his letter to declare that the men who translated the Bible into English were assisted by the same Spirit that inspired the Word in the first place. When it came to believing things about the Bible, McCraw expressed himself as follows:

1. *The Scotsman*, 1 June 1877.
2. See Black and Chrystal, *Life of William Robertson Smith*, pp. 229-34.

Now, surely nothing could be more awful than for any man to say that the book of Deuteronomy was not written by Moses? There is no difficulty in it at all to them that are, as they ought to be, able to believe all things, even as little children.

McCraw was not even worried by Moses writing about his own death. What was difficult about that for an inspired man?

But for me, one of the most telling parts of the letter is the quotation that I now give. When I first read it, part of it made me laugh and may make some of you laugh; but there is also something extremely important about it. Here is the extract:

did not my heart go with dear Dr Moody, when he lifted up his testimony in favour of the 'honoured name' of Solomon, against the profane supposition that he was capable of wishing to commit adultery...It may be true that he was not perfect before God, like his father, and that he loved many strange women who turned him to idolatry...But the Scriptures never say that he committed that sin which Dr Moody referred to. O no— he had no need to do that; he had 700 wives of his own and 300 concubines, and he was also the wisest of men.

McCraw's words here about Solomon were most likely a response to a sentence in Smith's article 'Bible' about the Song of Solomon where Smith quotes the view of 'most critics' that 'the pure love of the Shulamite for her betrothed is exhibited as victorious over the seduction of Solomon and his harem'.[3] Now, I am certain that Smith was *not* suggesting that Solomon had committed adultery; but these words could be read in that way by anyone intending to think badly of Smith. What is interesting here is the reference to Dr Moody, and its implication.

McCraw was referring to the American evangelist D.L. Moody who, with I.D. Sankey, had conducted an evangelistic campaign in Scotland from November 1873 to the summer of 1874. Its effect in the lowland cities of Scotland was considerable. According to the biographer of Robert Rainy,

Moody was in no sense a profound theologian, but he was a great human and a great Christian. He refreshed in Scotland the religious essentials of the Gospel—the love of God, the freeness of forgiveness, the power for holiness and, it should be added, the Christian call to righteousness and even philanthropy.[4]

3. W.R. Smith, 'Bible', in *Encyclopaedia Britannica* (9th edn, 1875), III, p. 639.
4. P. Carnegie Simpson, *The Life of Principal Rainy* (London: Hodder & Stoughton, 1909), I, pp. 408-409.

Hutchison in his recent *Political History of Scotland* writes:

> The reaction in Scottish cities was remarkable, and in Glasgow can justly
> be described as electrifying, with 3,000 converts being claimed...At a
> meeting in Ewing Place Church, 101 young men openly testified to their
> conversion, and this was followed by intense prayer sessions over a nine-
> month period, during which many more were converted.[5]

Hutchison goes on to describe the forming in 1874 of the Glasgow
United Evangelistic Association, part of whose work had a strong social
dimension, directed towards the poor, social outcasts, sleepers out and
destitute children.

The implication of all this for McCraw's letter to *The Scotsman* was
that the impact of Moody's work was a testimony to the truth of what
he said. Here was a man who had upheld the truth of the Bible, and
whose preaching had had its authority sealed by a religious awakening
that had not only brought many conversions but had impacted upon the
social and physical conditions of poor and destitute people. In the closing
paragraph of his letter McCraw was able to contrast Moody's defence of
Solomon and thus of Scripture with those who had impugned
Solomon's purity:

> Now where did that wicked supposition come from? From Germany, to be
> sure, that fountain of all poison, where these vain young men get them-
> selves spoiled, who wish to be wiser than their fathers...We leaned too
> much on human learning, and the Lord is now making us see again that it
> is the weak things and the foolish with which He chooses to confound the
> strong and the wise. O yes, and therefore I think the less we know of
> Hebrew in particular the better for ourselves, and for those who are
> committed to our care, and the less we meddle with questions of criticism
> and mere human ingenuity.

Alex McCraw's letter provoked further correspondence, and although
I am not primarily concerned with this, the sequel is worth noting for
the record. McCraw's letter was followed by one in which the corres-
pondent suggested that German should join Hebrew as a prohibited
language in the Free Church colleges. Not to be outdone, Peter
McCraw, a cousin of Alex, wrote to *The Scotsman* on 8 June 1877
concerning the banning of German:

---

5.   J.G.C. Hutchison, *A Political History of Scotland 1832–1924: Parties,
Elections and Issues* (Edinburgh: John Donald, 1986), p. 137.

I think no wise person will deny that, and Latin and Greek also, and French too.

One language that would not be banned, however, was Gaelic; and indeed Peter McCraw was inclined to judge the leaders of his church by whether, and how well, they knew Gaelic![6] He concluded:

> That vain curiosity and undependence [*sic*], and logic and metaphysics, and science and philosophy, and Greek and Hebrew, and French and German, must all be stamped out together. What are *we*, poor creatures, to take upon us to say anything beyond what is written, and which all the best men that went before us believed?[7]

This quotation brings us to the heart of the subject of this lecture. What should our attitude be to the controversy that changed the course of Smith's life so fundamentally? It is easy to laugh at the man who wanted to stamp out altogether all science, philosophy and ancient and modern languages. It is easy to regard Smith as the hero of an attempt to bring the Free Church into the modern world, and to regard his opponents as obscurantist or self-seeking.

Donald Carswell in his entertaining book *Brother Scots* depicts James Begg as a truculent and vindictive bully whose influence in the councils of the church was won and maintained by a system of terrorism and coarse intrigue. 'As a pushful, money-making Lanarkshire farmer Begg would have done well and might have passed for a useful member of society; but as an ecclesiastic it does not appear that he ever in all his

6.   Peter McCraw to *The Scotsman*, 8 June 1877: 'There is another who I thought had more judgement at one time—Professor Macgregor, for he has the Gaelic. But it's a poor sort of Gaelic he has, and it's no wonder therefore that he is going wrong. [Lindsay] had too much philosophy altogether, and German and Dutch, and every bad language, and he had no Gaelic. Who would expect anything else of him but what he is?' Peter McCraw's view of life is also illustrated by the following words in his letter: 'there are those that wouldn't believe in evil spirits, even if they saw lights and heard chains clanking, in the middle of a peat moss at dead of night, as I have done.'

7.   Peter McCraw's brother, Lachlan McCraw, wrote to *The Scotsman* on 12 June to put a different view: 'It's not for nothing that I spent the best of my days on the other side of the globe. What a pity that our clergymen couldn't be sent, every man jack of them, for a few years to learn something of the world in other countries. That would be better for them than any amount of Hebrew or even of Gaelic!...Talk about being like little children. They don't even know the meaning of their Master's words. We are to be as little children in *spirit*, but not in *intellect*. Are they so? On the contrary, they are babies in intellect, but as old tyrannical Inquisitors in spirit.'

ministry of fifty-odd years devised or did anything but mischief.'[8]

Carswell is kinder to Robert Rainy, although he cannot resist two small digs. The first refers to Rainy's habit of making fine distinctions. In reply to the question whether a committee should omit a controversial clause from a draft document that was being discussed, Rainy is said to have replied 'No, we shall simply not include it'. The other dig is a reference to a hostile newspaper that spoke of 'the curious mind of Principal Rainy worming like a corkscrew through material soft enough to be perforated by a chisel thrust'.[9] With verdicts such as these, it is easy to think of the Robertson Smith affair as a case of truth versus ignorance, sincerity versus deviousness and sacrifice versus self-preservation. Even Smith's verdict on Rainy, in a letter to his friend and biographer J.S. Black dated 14 February 1880, strengthens this view. Smith wrote:

> I don't think that slimy cold blooded reptile Rainy will stop till he has got the whole Church into a hole from which it can't get out again. He must be assassinated.[10]

However, for the next part of this lecture I intend to come to the rescue of Begg and Rainy; not in order to denigrate Smith, but in order to set the remaining five lectures in a context other than that of supposing that Smith was merely and rightly combatting, but victim to, obscurantism and deviousness.

In Stewart Mechie's Cunningham Lectures given in Edinburgh in 1957 and entitled *The Church and Scottish Social Development 1780–1870* there is a whole chapter devoted to James Begg.[11] In this chapter one sees a quite different Begg from the one associated with the Robertson Smith case. That Begg perhaps bears some resemblance to Donald Carswell's cruel portrait: a diehard opponent of union with the United Presbyterians, of any form of biblical criticism, and of any kind of musical instrument in church. Yet, as Mechie remarks, had Begg been killed and not merely injured in a railway accident in which he was involved in 1865, his name would have gone down in history as that of an early and zealous social reformer.[12]

8. D. Carswell, *Brother Scots* (London: Constable, 2nd impression, 1927), p. 72.

9. *Brother Scots*, p. 74.

10. W.R. Smith to J.S. Black, 14 February 1880, Cambridge University Library ADD 7449 A 70.

11. S. Mechie, *The Church and Scottish Social Development 1780–1870* (London: Oxford University Press, 1960), pp. 119-35.

12. Mechie, *Church and Scottish Social Development*, p. 119. The standard

The portrait that emerges from Mechie's account would do justice to an Old Testament prophet. It is easy to think of Begg as an Amos denouncing the social ills of his day, with the difference that whereas Amos expected the judgment of God to come swiftly upon Israel, Begg was able to play a modest role in eliminating some of the social ills that he denounced.

The worst ills were, of course, in the cities, as a result of the industrial revolution. Thomas Brown's moving book *Annals of the Disruption* describes some of the awful conditions in parts of Edinburgh and Glasgow which were early targeted by the young Free Church, led by men such as Chalmers and McColl. In West Port, Edinburgh, around 1844 there was a population of

> two thousand, of whom fifteen hundred had no connection with any Christian Church, living chiefly in filthy closes where drunkenness and vice prevailed. There were four hundred and fifty children of school age, two hundred and ninety of whom were growing up untaught and utterly neglected.[13]

In a district of Glasgow known as 'The Wynds' twelve thousand people were crammed into twelve acres in conditions that were ideal for typhus and cholera. The Revd Mr McColl, who devoted himself to this district, wrote that there were

> many dark devious dens to which the thief and the harlot, like beasts of prey, could retire, and from which, as night came down, they might creep forth and seek their prey. The sober, industrious inhabitants left the place—whisky shops multiplied—there were the wild orgies of Saturday night, and the saturnalia of the Glasgow fair; and in the midst of these evil influences, 'The Wynds' were getting worse and worse every year.[14]

It was in about 1840 that Begg made a personal inspection of the areas of Edinburgh and Glasgow just described. He was then in his early thirties, and he subsequently spent thirty-five years addressing himself to remedying what he had seen.[15] His activities took various forms. First, there was the matter of gaining information, and it is noteworthy that a

biography of Begg, T. Smith, *Memoirs of James Begg, DD* (Edinburgh, 1885–88) does not emphasize Begg's social concerns.

13. T. Brown, *Annals of the Disruption; with Extracts from the Narratives of Ministers who left the Scottish Establishment in 1843* (Edinburgh, 1884), p. 736.

14. Brown, *Annals*, p. 740.

15. For this, and what follows, see Mechie, *Church and Scottish Social Development*, pp. 122-30.

Committee on the Housing of the Working Classes, set up by the General Assembly of the Free Church in 1858 on Begg's urging, and chaired by him, was largely instrumental in getting inserted in the census forms for Scotland for the national census of 1861 a question about the number of rooms in each dwelling house. This question, familiar nowadays to all of us who have completed a census form, was not in 1861 included for England and Ireland. The results of the 1861 census on this point were shocking, revealing that a third of the entire population of Scotland lived in one-roomed houses. Of these one-roomed houses, nearly twenty per cent (over 40,000) had from six to sixteen occupants. In Glasgow, some 100,000 of the population lived in one-roomed houses, with over 2000 of them having from seven to fifteen occupants.

Secondly, Begg tried to stir up interest in the country in general and his church in particular in the matter of working-class housing. Not only did he address the General Assembly and local meetings, but he also spoke in 1857 at the first annual meeting of the Social Science Association in Birmingham, and in 1866 published a book with the today quaint-sounding title *Happy Homes for Working Men*.[16] Thirdly, Begg tried to get changes made to the legal infrastructure that made it difficult for land to be acquired for building new homes. Apparently, the law of entail whereby land could be willed to a number of inheritors, together with complicated procedures of conveyancing, prevented land from becoming easily available. Further, whereas in England there was an incentive for people to acquire small lots of land and to build their houses, thereby qualifying as parliamentary electors, no such provision existed in Scotland.

Fourthly, Begg played a leading role in the establishment of the Edingburgh Co-operative Building Company in 1861.[17] This was an enterprise whose aim was to enable working men to build their own houses. Its basic idea was simple. As houses were built they were rented to working men, but the rents did not go to landlords but to two objectives. First, the rents went to the Co-operative to finance the building of more houses; and secondly, the rents paid off the purchase price so that usually in about fourteen years a tenant became the outright owner. In a matter of ten years, over 900 houses were built in this fashion, admittedly a drop in the ocean compared with the overall housing problem, but a practical response to it which, had it been widely

16. Begg, *Happy Homes for Working Men, and How to Get Them* (London [?], 1866).

17. Mechie, *Church and Scottish Social Development*, pp. 130-32.

adopted, could have made more of an impact.

So far, I have mentioned only Begg's concern for the city-dwelling working classes. But he was also interested in the agricultural workers, and was particularly incensed by the bothy system. The bothy was a rather gruesome dwelling provided for agricultural workers by their employers. The workers were expected to remain unmarried and to live crowded together in their quarters. Begg described the bothy as

> a kind of human stable or cow-house, invented for cheapness by the greedy lairds of Aberdeen and Angus, into which the farm labourers, made in the image of God, are huddled after their work.

He continued

> Landlords should be plainly told, and especially our Scotch landlords, that the very least thing they can do is to build decent cottages for those by the sweat of whose brows their rents are secured.[18]

What, then, were Begg's reasons for devoting so much of his time and energy to working-class housing? Clearly, there was a humanitarian element; but most powerfully, Begg was driven by biblical principles. He followed what today would be called 'creation ethics', that is, the belief that the Bible reveals God's will for the way in which human society should be ordered so as to be in harmony with the created order. Among the creation ordinances was the family, and Begg reckoned that if the family was God's gift to humanity, then agricultural workers living in their bothies had the right to be married, and that married people had the right to homes that were not an affront to God's purposes.

Begg wrote in his *Happy Homes for Working Men*:

> the family system, like the Sabbath law, being an institution of Paradise, is essentially connected with the permanent well-being of man. No mere extension of barrack accommodation will therefore cure the evil that exists. Man must not only have a covering but a *home*. God made men in families; and it is upon the right maintenance and ordering of these little kingdoms that the peace and social order of all the great kingdoms of the world depends.[19]

Begg was, of course, too convinced an evangelical to suppose that simply by altering the social conditions of people they would necessarily be better or Christian. But he saw clearly the converse: that people were

---

18. Mechie, *Church and Scottish Social Development*, p. 125.
19. Begg, *Happy Homes for Working Men*, p. iv.

unlikely to be better and Christian if they lived in intolerable conditions. Thus, he castigated a church that seemed to think that being indifferent to social conditions was a virtue, and we almost certainly hear his voice in the following words of a report to the Assembly of the Free Church in 1862:

> a spiritual canker has invaded many in the Protestant Church—not only the idea that the ministers of Christ have nothing to do with such so-called secular matters of the houses of the people, but that to manifest an utter indifference upon the whole subject is a mark of superior sanctity. To our mind this is not simply a reversal of the whole spirit of the Bible and the Reformation, it is a 'glorying in our shame'.[20]

All this had, of course political implications, and Begg's ideal was for a property-owning Christian democracy, but one in which there would be a multiplication of Bethels: 'houses in which the fear and worship of God shall be found'.[21]

It is also interesting to note that Begg was associated with the stirrings of Scottish nationalism in the 1850s.[22] He believed that some of the problems to be found in Scotland resulted from its neglect by the Westminster parliament. He believed that there should be a Secretary of State for Scotland and even possibly a Scottish Legislative body.[23] We are a long way from Donald Carswell's observation that, in fifty-odd years of ministry, Begg had done nothing but devise mischief.[24]

What has this to do with Robertson Smith? My intention has been to put the Smith case into a much more serious context. As long as we regard men such as James Begg as ignorant buffoons who opposed the use of organs in churches, we shall not take the issues seriously. By the time that Begg became one of the leaders of the opposition against Smith (he was born in 1808 and was thus 68 when proceedings against Smith began in 1876), he had long been marginalized in the Free Church, and had become more obstructive than helpful in many issues,

20. Mechie, *Church and Scottish Social Development*, p. 128.
21. Mechie, *Church and Scottish Social Development*, p. 134.
22. Hutchison, *Political History*, p. 92.
23. Mechie, *Church and Scottish Social Development*, p. 121.
24. The picture of Begg provided by Mechie shows how inadequate Carswell's treatment is. It is therefore unfortunate when writers such as T.O. Beidelman commend Carswell's work without warning readers of its shortcomings. See T.O. Beidelman, *W. Robertson Smith and the Sociological Study of Religion* (Chicago: University of Chicago Press, 1974), p. 70.

as witness his implacable opposition to union with the United Presbyterians.[25] Yet I, for one, cannot doubt the profound sincerity of his opposition to Smith. For it was not simply a clash of intellectual ideas that was taking place; something much deeper was at issue. Begg, we have seen, had devoted over thirty years of his life to the cause of working-class housing because he believed that the creation ordinance of the family indicated God's will for the material as well as the spiritual well-being of the human race. He also based some of his views on the Ten Commandments. In Smith's article 'Bible' he found something that was as alien as could possibly be to all that he had believed and fought for. Instead of an article that told the general public what the Bible taught about the requirements of God, he read page after page of material that dwelt upon the human aspect of the Bible; he read of sources, of duplicate narratives, of the fusion of narratives and of final redactors; he read that the prophets were not primarily writers and that what we have of their words is probably greatly abridged; he read that the editors of Psalms made verbal changes to their texts and composed new psalms out of fragments of older ones. Smith could plead with all his might that he was a committed evangelical seeking to do justice to the Bible in the light of modern knowledge. For a man such as Begg, this would be quite unintelligible, not necessarily out of ignorance or cussedness, but because of a clash of two cultures.

But at this stage we must avoid going to an opposite extreme. Having described Begg's commitment to working-class housing, it would be easy to pit the socially-active Begg over against the academic and non-practical Smith. We could hear the echoes in advance of the complaint that liberation theologians from South America have sometimes made against Western biblical scholarship, to the effect that it is detached from reality and is thus deaf to the authentic message of the Old Testament. This, however, would also be a mistake. We must remind ourselves that Smith held his professorship in Aberdeen not in the university but in the Free Church College, and that he fully understood his responsibilities to the College and his church. He was not a frustrated academic who was serving his time in a church college and waiting for the first opportunity to get out of it into a university academic post. It is true that Smith was pressed to apply for a mathematics chair in Glasgow in 1880 and that Harvard offered him a chair, also in 1880.[26] But Smith was not willing

25. See Carnegie Simpson, *Life of Rainy*, I, pp. 161-74.
26. See Black and Chrystal, *Life of William Robertson Smith*, pp. 327, 340-42.

to abandon his responsibilities to his church. Indeed, if we examine Smith's letters and sermons we get a strong sense of the high degree of pastoral responsibility that he possessed as well as his concern for social matters.

In 1870 Smith had translated a brief extract from Albrecht Ritschl's great work on the Christian Doctrine of Justification for the magazine *The Presbyterian*. Ritschl was quite amused by Smith's choice of material from the book, which, as he wrote to Smith, displayed a high sense of pastoral wisdom, and made Ritschl appear to be very Calvinist.[27] Again, in his sermons, one of Smith's recurring themes was the kingdom of God, by means of which he emphasized that Christianity was not just a matter of the commitment of individual believers to Jesus Christ, but the fellowship of believers and of their love to each other. His sermons also indicate a concern for the social implications of the gospel. Thus, in a sermon on words from Rom. 5.20-21: 'where sin abounded, grace did much more abound', Smith said:

> The blackest sides of society in the days before the gospel are so dark that we dare not lift the veil from them; but if you consider that till Christianity came there was not in all the civilised world one charitable institution—that sick slaves were habitually cast out into the streets to starve—that infanticide was no crime—that the death of unoffending captives by each others' hands was the favourite spectacle of the people, it will hardly be necessary to adduce the yet stronger proofs of moral degradation that might easily be brought.[28]

It is also the case, as I shall explain in my second lecture, that Smith had made a detailed study of the German scholar Richard Rothe's *Ethics* and that he had written on Rothe's view of the relations betweeen church and state.[29]

In contrasting Smith and Begg, then, we must avoid seeing them as the social reformer versus the academic intellectual, just as we must avoid

27. Smith to J.S. Black, 31 January 1871, where he says that he has found time 'to write a short notice and/or rather to translate an extract from Ritschl's book for *The Presbyterian*. Ritschl is amused by the "hohen Grad von Pastoralweisheit" shown in the relation of his passage which "klingt so als ob ich ein eingefleischter Calvinist wäre"', Cambridge University Library ADD 7449 A16. For Smith's relationship with Ritschl see below pp. 77-81.

28. W.R. Smith, Sermon on Rom. 5.20-1, preached eight times between 1 May 1870 and 3 November 1822, Cambridge University Library ADD 7449 K29.

29. W.R. Smith to his father, 3 December 1869, Cambridge University Library ADD 7449 C127.

the stereotypes of obscurantist buffoon versus the enlightened critic.

At this point I intend to turn to the social theory of the German socio-logist Richard Münch in order to approach the matter from a different angle.[30] I would like to think that Smith would approve of this, given his much-praised pioneering contribution to the sociological study of religion. Münch uses systems theory to study how subsystems within larger systems function in relation to each other and how logic and rationality play their part in this. For our purposes we can say that the Free Church of Scotland was a system within Münch's definition, that is, a self-referential institution within the larger society. We can also identify subsystems within the institution, such as parishes, presbyteries and the colleges. With regard to the colleges we can note that they, of all the subsystems, were the most open to outside influences, and indeed that their self-definition depended as much upon the self-definition of international academic professional institutions as upon their location within the Free Church.

Münch describes a number of conceivable constellations of how sub-systems relate to each other, of which the following two are relevant to this discussion:

1. The subsystems are strongly developed, but the mediating systems are poorly developed: the result is conflict.
2. One subsystem is strongly developed, but the others and the mediating systems are poorly developed: the result is the dominance of that one subsystem over others.[31]

Of these two constellations, the first is probably the more appropriate to the Robertson Smith case. Subsystems such as parishes and the colleges were strongly developed in their particular ways and the mediating systems, that is, the debating and voting type representative gatherings at local, regional and national level were not suitable mechanisms for resolving conflicts between them. There is, of course, the complicating

---

30. R. Münch's major works include *Die Struktur der Moderne: Grundmuster und differentielle Gestaltung des institutionelle Aufbaus der modernen Gesellschaften* (Frankfurt: Suhrkamp, 1984); *Die Kultur der Moderne. I. Ihre Grundlagen und ihre Entwicklung in England und Amerika* (Frankfurt: Suhrkamp, 1986); *Die Kultur der Moderne. II. Ihre Entwicklung in Frankreich und Deutschland* (Frankfurt: Suhrkamp, 1986). The examples in this lecture are taken from his article 'Parsonian Theory Today: In Search of a New Synthesis', in A. Giddens and J. Turner (eds.), *Social Theory Today* (Cambridge: Polity Press, 1987), pp. 116-55.

31. Münch, 'Parsonian Theory', p. 127.

factor that opinions about biblical criticism were divided in the colleges and the parishes, without there being effective mediating systems to resolve these conflicts.

Of mediating systems, Münch defines the following and then makes a general observation.

1. Exchange produces open and unstable integration (that is, as I understand it, exchange of people or factors between subsystems undermines the strongly self-determining features of the subsystems and leads to an unstable integration of vaguely-defined subsystems).
2. Authority causes integration which is compulsively enforced domination.
3. Communal association leads to a conformist and immobile integration. (I take it that the problem here is lack of any proper rationale for integration).
4. Discourse implies integration through reconciliation.
5. The combination of exchange, authority, communal association and discourse...is the main pre-condition for the inter-penetration of strongly-developed subsystems.[32]

Münch describes social change as follows:

> we can take cultural patterns to be a genetic code which during the process of sociocultural evolution obeys, *internally*, a logic of rational argument and...approaches a cultural pattern with increasingly universal validity. *Externally*, this cultural pattern has to be converted into particular institutional patterns by interpretative procedures.[33]

We can apply this to the Smith case as follows. To use Münch's terminology, the Britain and Western Europe of the nineteenth century were changing rapidly in response to the logic of new scientific advances and their application to technology—a technology, for example, that was eliminating common killer diseases by providing proper water supplies and sanitation to name one minor, but vital, item. But how would these changes be institutionalized and, above all, how would they be interpreted? Would they be interpreted in a way that left God completely out of account, or would they be set in an interpretative framework in which the church would play a decisive role? If there was to be

---

32. Münch, 'Parsonian Theory', p. 127.
33. Münch, 'Parsonian Theory', p. 137.

an interpretative framework in which the church played a central role, who would provide and communicate that interpretative framework? One thing was certain; it would not be provided in Britain, where, until the late 1880s at least, the churches were too concerned with stemming the tide of liberal thought to be able to think of a new synthesis and where, in any case, there was no strong tradition of innovative or creative theology.[34]

The one place where there was such a tradition was Protestant Germany. A combination of the German speculative philosophical tradition, the political questions raised by the final defeat of Napoleon and by the revolution of 1848, and the question of German unity all kept to the forefront the relation between church and society, and biblical scholars and theologians such as Ewald, Bunsen and Rothe, to name but three, took an active part in politics in different ways. Further, we must never forget the far greater amount of theological activity in Germany as compared with Britain. Throughout the nineteenth century there were twenty Protestant theological faculties in Germany, while in Britain there were five ancient universities in Scotland and only two in England plus some foundations from around 1830.[35] The combined theological endeavour of the British institutions, including the Free Church and Nonconformist academies, came nowhere near the achievements of their German counterparts.

Whereas in Germany a sustained theological debate about the relation between church and society continued throughout the nineteenth century,[36] in Britain there was a change of perspective in what a large number of educated people believed or found believable about the world, which amounted to a reinterpretation of reality which left the church out of account. This changing creed has been described by James R. Moore as follows.[37] In 1830 educated people in Britain believed in a static world of nature created by God, a static and unequal society ruled by people who had an inherited right to rule, a static moral order whose

---

34. See further my comments in *Old Testament Criticism*, pp. 8-11.

35. See the table of German Protestant Theological faulties in Rogerson, *Old Testament Criticism*, pp. 142-44. In counting the Scottish universities I have taken King's College and Marischall College in Aberdeen as two universities.

36. See F.W. Graf, 'Kulturprotestantismus', in *TRE*, XX (Berlin: de Gruyter, 1990), pp. 230-43.

37. J.R. Moore, 'Freethought, Secularism, Agnosticism: The Case of Charles Darwin', in G. Parsons (ed.), *Religion in Victorian Britain*. I. *Traditions* (Manchester: Manchester University Press, 1988), pp. 274-319, esp. p. 277.

rules were provided by the Bible and the church, and a hope of improvement only in terms of a world to come after death, a world that was attained by obedient submission to whatever, in the will of God, might befall one. By 1880 that had changed to belief in a nature that was evolving, a society that was progressing away from hereditary inequality to natural inequality (the right of the fittest to rule), a progressive moral order whose rules were provided as much by scientific professionals as by the church, and a hope in terms of an improved present material world overcoming and eliminating evils that were once thought to be the will of God. Crusades such as those of Moody and Sankey, while having tangible results, could only reinforce those aspects of general belief that were being abandoned by educated people; the same was true of all atempts in all churches to resist new knowledge, including biblical criticism.

It is not surprising that Smith turned to Protestant German thought to enable him to sustain his evangelical beliefs in the light of new knowledge, and to find an interpretative framework that put new knowledge and new developments in society under the lordship of Christ.[38] Nor is it surprising that he believed that he could teach his church what he described in a letter to the great Dutch scholar, Abraham Kuenen, as the alphabet of criticism.[39] He no doubt entertained the equally sincere conviction that the theology of his church could respond to the new challenges of the nineteenth century in the way that was being attempted in Germany. In this he was mistaken; but his mistake is not to be judged as naive optimism, nor should the attitudes of his opponents be seen in terms of obscurantism or self-interest.

Their attitudes have often been described in this way. We have heard, and have had seen good reasons for rejecting, Donald Carswell's devastating verdict on James Begg. Of Principal Robert Rainy it has been said that he sacrificed Smith in order to maintain the unity of the Free Church and also to ensure his continued supremacy within it.[40] But if we look at the matter in terms of Münch's theory of how institutions function as systems, we gain a different perspective. The fact is, and this is not meant to be a criticism, that the Free Church did not possess the mediating mechanisms that would allow rational discourse to play its

38. See Chapter 5.

39. W.R. Smith to Abraham Kuenen, 10 June 1880, Leiden University Library, BPL 3028.

40. Cf. Carswell, *Brother Scots*, p. 118.

part in reconciling differences and in producing a new interpretative rationale in terms of which the institution could understand itself in a changing world. We need to consider this from the point of view of Smith, Begg and Rainy.

As an academic, Smith was very familiar with rational discourse as a method of achieving understanding and, in some cases, integration. Indeed, the extent to which Smith was able to agree on critical matters with scholars such as Wellhausen and Kuenen, whose theological views differed so fundamentally from his own, has sometimes been misunderstood to the point of thinking that Smith modified or gave up his own Christian beliefs. Within his college, in spite of differences of opinion among its members of staff, he belonged to a subsystem which was open to outside influences in a way matched by no other subsystem within his church. When he was called upon to defend his views before the General Assembly, however, his defence could not take the form of rational discussion. His defence had to conform to the rules of adversarial argument against quasi-legal charges in a forum which, as Smith's biographers remarked,

> is in any case unfitted for the conduct of judicial proceedings, but eminently so when the questions at issue are not questions of ordinary morality, but difficult questions of scholarship and theology, requiring for a right decision the equipment of a scholar and the trained and unbiassed intelligence of a judge.[41]

From James Begg's angle we can say that his experience of the church was in terms of the mediating mechanism in which authority causes integration which is compulsively enforced domination. In Hutchison's *Political History of Scotland* it is noted that, from the 1850s, Begg was constantly outvoted on a whole series of issues concerning the internal affairs of the Free Church, as Robert Candlish became its leader supported by Drs Buchanan and Cunningham as the top administrators of the Free Church. Hutchison quotes from Begg's 1855 pamphlet *The Crisis in the Free Church*, in which Begg declared:

> Probably there is no corporation in Britain so despotically governed at this moment as the Free Church of Scotland. A limited number of men notoriously manage all our affairs in any way they please…The Free Church is as completely managed by an oligarchy as ever the British government was.[42]

41. Black and Chrystal, *Life of William Robertson Smith*, pp. 362-63.
42. Hutchison, *Political History*, p. 92.

Given this view, and his increasing sense of marginalization, Begg's main recourse was to the General Assembly, that authoritative body which, in Münch's terms, integrated by means of compulsively enforced domination, where he played an increasingly obstructive role. From his standpoint, the outcome of the Robertson Smith case was a rare triumph.

This brings me to Robert Rainy, Smith's cold-blooded reptile, who succeeded Robert Candlish as the leader of the Free Church. Rainy would not have agreed with Begg that the Free Church was despotically governed. Indeed, Rainy had been the hero of the hour in 1872 when he publically rebutted an English episcopalian who had dared to lecture to Scots about their ecclesiastical affairs; I refer to Dean Stanley who lectured on the Scottish Church in Edinburgh in January 1872. In his reply to Stanley, Rainy maintained among other things:

> Presbyterianism meant organised life, regulated distribution of forces, graduated recognition of gifts, freedom to discuss, authority to control, agency to administer. Presbyterianism meant a system by which the convictions and conscience of the Church could constantly be applied, by appropriate organs to her current affairs…From the broad base of the believing people, the sap rose through sessions, Presbyteries, Synods, to the Assembly, and thence descending diffused knowledge, influence, unanimity through the whole system.[43]

One is tempted to wonder whether this statement is similar to modern-day university Annual Reports which describe institutions that can scarcely be recognized by those who work in them. Or perhaps Rainy enjoyed that detachment from real life that enabled him to believe sincerely that he presided over an institution that encouraged freedom of discussion and achieved unanimity through the whole system. Whatever motivated his behaviour in the Smith affair, Rainy perceived, whether consciously or not, that the mediating mechanisms of his church were not adequate to cope with the implications of the questions raised by Smith. The explanation that he sacrified Smith in order to safeguard the unity of the institution is a convincing explanation from this standpoint.

However, I think that the time is past for judging Begg and Rainy or even McCraw adversely. They were all doing what they believed to be right in a situation where, through nobody's fault, the institutions that they served did not know how to cope with the enormous changes in knowledge and culture that the nineteenth century was bringing about.

43. Carnegie Simpson, *Life of Rainy*, p. 229. The whole of chapter 9 is devoted to 'The Tourney with Dean Stanley'.

For the remainder of these lectures I shall concentrate entirely upon that other culture, the one emanating from Germany but interpreted by Smith, which tried to respond on behalf of theology to the massive changes of the nineteenth century. It is part of the genius of William Robertson Smith that he, perhaps more clearly than anyone else in Victorian Britain, saw the nature of the challenge, and devoted his life to trying to meet it.

Chapter 5

THE GERMAN CONNECTION

'If Mr Casaubon read German he would save himself a great deal of trouble.'

'I do not understand you,' said Dorothea, startled and anxious.

'I merely mean,' said Will, in an offhand way, 'that the Germans have taken the lead in historical inquiries, and they laugh at results which are got by groping about in the woods with a pocket compass while they have made good roads.'...

Dorothea raised her eyes, brighter than usual with excited feeling, and said, in her saddest recitative, 'How I wish I had learned German when I was at Lausanne! There were plenty of German teachers. But now I can be of no use.'[1]

George Eliot's *Middlemarch* appeared in 1871–72 at the beginning of Smith's tenure of his post at the Free Church College. We know from a letter that Smith wrote to John Sutherland Black from Aberdeen on 17 July 1874 that Smith had read *Middlemarch*, and that it had made him angry. He declared: 'The whole lesson of the book is that the world is without any true moral unity and purpose. Any idealism there is is false.'[2] Although Smith disliked what he took to be the lesson of *Middlemarch* he would have agreed thoroughly with the point that its author was making about the importance of German. Marian Lewes (alias George Eliot) knew what she was talking about. Not only had she translated D.F. Strauss's *Life of Jesus* into English; her common-law husband George Henry Lewes (with whom Smith corresponded on matters mathematical) was the author of a work on the life of Goethe.[3]

1.   G. Eliot, *Middlemarch* (The Penguin English Library; Harmondsworth: Penguin, 1965), p. 240.

2.   W.R. Smith to J.S. Black, 17 July 1874, Cambridge University Library ADD 7449 A 25.

3.   G.H. Lewes, *The Life and Works of Goethe* (London, 1855). For correspondence between Lewes and Smith see Cambridge University Library ADD

Smith began his study of German at the age of nineteen, between November 1865 and April 1866, in preparation for his studies at the New College, Edinburgh, which began in October 1866.[4] In the spring of 1867, having completed his first session in Edinburgh, Smith made his first visit to Germany to improve his German and to expose himself to German theology.[5] Because, to quote his biographers, 'he felt some hesitation in exposing himself to the most rationalistic teaching in Germany',[6] he went to Bonn. This was a university whose theological faculty accepted the critical method in biblical studies but within the context of more conservative results.[7] Even so, Smith found himself confronted with positions that were radical in comparison with what was found in Britain. Importantly, he began to discover that some people who would be written off as rationalists in Britain were in fact sincere believers.

One of the Old Testament scholars whom Smith heard and met in Bonn was Adolf Kamphausen, who is best known for having completed Bunsen's massive *Bibelwerk für die Gemeinde*.[8] Smith described his encounters with Kamphausen as follows:

> I found him rationalistic, as we should say, that is, he holds for example that a passage of S[acred] S[cripture] can contain no more for us than for the author, and that its full meaning is to be obtained by placing ourselves at the author's standpoint. At the same time, though this view leads him to admit that there may be historical errors in the Bible, and to refer Daniel to the period of the Maccabees, etc, he is not a rationalist according to the Germans, who reserve that name for those who deny supernatural inspiration and prophecy altogether. The middle position of K[amphausen] I do not fully understand and may not have done justice to. Certainly the

7449 D400-405. George Eliot's knowledge of German and German literature is detailed by A. McCobb, *George Eliot's Knowledge of German Life and Letters* (Salzburg Studies in English Literature: Romantic Reassessment, 102.2; Salzburg: Institut für Anglistik und Amerikanistik der Universität Salzburg, 1982). I am grateful to Professor J.M. Ritchie for this last reference.

4. See the *Memorandum* of Smith's father, William Pirie Smith, Cambridge University Library ADD 7476 M, p. 29.

5. Pirie Smith, *Memorandum*, p. 31.

6. Black and Chrystal, *Life of William Robertson Smith*, p. 85.

7. Rogerson, *Old Testament Criticism*, p. 139.

8. Rogerson, *Old Testament Criticism*, p. 129.

language in which he spoke of the Messianic Psalms today seems very
much orthodox. I must repeat, however, that I do not follow his lectures
well enough to speak with certainty.[9]

This observation was written to his father on 8 May 1867. On 10 July
1867 he wrote:

> I went a long walk [sic] with Professor Kamphausen and had a great deal
> of interesting conversation with him, especially on Inspiration, a subject on
> which he is very far from orthodox. At the same time he is a very sincere
> and, I believe, pious man; in fact, it is quite absurd to regard the heterodox
> Germans as infidels. Of course, I do not mean that such men as Strauss
> are not infidels. But Kamphausen, though in regard to some points very
> heterodox (e.g. he goes about as far as Colenso on the Pentateuch
> question), is on other points, I may say, strictly orthodox. So far as I can
> see, he holds quite orthodox views on the person, miracles, etc., of Christ,
> and lays special weight on the *testimonium Spiritus Sancti.* [10]

In May of 1869, Smith paid his second visit to Germany in order to
spend a semester in Göttingen.[11] Here, he attended the lectures of
Hermann Lotze on metaphysics, Albrecht Ritschl on theological ethics
and Ernst Bertheau on Old Testament theology.[12] Bertheau had taken
up his chair in Göttingen after Ewald's departure to Tübingen, but we
have no record of his impact, if any, on Smith. Lotze, on the other hand,
was regarded as one of the leading philosophers in Germany of his time,
in contrast to his great neglect today. His importance in the second half
of the nineteenth century, and the reason for his neglect today, was that
he worked at a time when the idealist philosophy of the first part of the
nineteenth century was being replaced by the realist or materialist
philosophy of the second part of that century. Lotze sought to combine
both approaches into a system that was fundamentally empirical in its
observation and interpretation of history and the material world, yet
which interpreted the whole of reality in terms of value and worth. His
two-volume work *Microcosmos* is a noble attempt to describe the
physical constitution and development of the universe and of the human

9.   Black and Chrystal, *Life of William Robertson Smith*, p. 87.

10.   Black and Chrystal, *Life of William Robertson Smith*, p. 88.

11.   Black and Chrystal (*Life of William Robertson Smith*, pp. 111-14) give a brief
account of the visit. There is fuller information in Smith's letters to his father.

12.   Smith to his father on 24 May 1869, Cambridge University Library ADD
7449 C116a.

race in terms of an ascent to its highest understanding in Christianity.[13]

We know that Smith kept in touch with Lotze, and that when Smith was a candidate for the chair at the Free Church College in 1870 Lotze, 'in the course of a very strongly worded letter, regretted that Germany might not have the chance of claiming him entirely for her own'.[14] The direct influence of Lotze upon Smith is impossible to trace. Lotze's views on Christianity were different from Smith's. But the similarity between the two men that has struck me is that both were at one and the same time idealists and realists. Although this is something that will become apparent later in these lectures, Smith was an idealist when he wrote about Hebrew prophecy and a realist when he wrote about Semitic polytheism. Further, he combined the two approaches in such a way as to see in the pre-prophetic religion of Israel, which had much in common with Semitic polytheism, evidences of God's grace at work. Thus, although direct influence of Lotze upon Smith cannot be demonstrated, it is not unreasonable to suggest that Lotze's system enabled Smith to see how idealism and realism could be combined.

Of greater importance to Smith was the presence in Göttingen of Albrecht Ritschl. Ritschl (1822–1889) had been in Göttingen since 1864, and had once been an adherent of the radical Tübingen hypothesis of the origins of the New Testament.[15] Having rejected that approach, he now advocated a theology that was neither philosophical nor confessional, but biblical. One of his great works, on the history of justification, sought to see the grace of God as directed specifically towards the believing community, rather than individuals, and he expressed the doctrine of justification in terms of its outworking in the kingdom of God envisaged as a moral community. The following quotation gives the flavour of these convictions:

> At Christmas I want to hear that we are the *anthropoi eudokias*, the chosen community of this child…on Good Friday I want to hear that we are the community founded by the fully-completed reconciliation (*Versöhnung*),

13. H. Lotze, *Microcosmos: An Essay concerning Man and his Relation to the World* (2 vols.; Edinburgh, 1897).

14. Black and Chrystal, *Life of William Robertson Smith*, p. 119.

15. See O. Ritschl, *Albrecht Ritschls Leben* (2 vols.; Freiburg im Breisgau, 1892–96).

at Easter, that we are the community that Christ has taken with him out of death and has set down with him in heaven in order to rule the world through it...[16]

On 24 May 1869 Smith wrote to his father:

I have never heard anything as interesting on a theological subject as Ritschl's lectures. He has evidently such thorough clearness in his own views and such complete acquaintance with the views of others as to make his lectures exceedingly instructive.[17]

On 12 August 1868 he wrote:

Ritschl and Lotze closed yesterday...Ritschl has been very profitable [;] far the best course of lectures I ever heard.[18]

As a result of this visit, Smith began an acquaintance with this German professor nearly twenty-five years his elder that was more than formal. Ritschl wanted Smith to translate the first volume of his work on justification into English, and although Smith refused, he did agree to advise his friend and later biographer J.S. Black, who undertook the task.[19] Smith felt that Ritschl's views should be better known in Scotland, to which end he published a review of the first volume of the work on Justification in *The Presbyterian* in 1871, including an extract from the work.[20] Contact between the two continued and, not unnaturally, intensified during the time of Smith's trials. The trials, indeed, bring to our notice a piece of information which is both intriguing and yet hard to evalute.

16. O. Ritschl, *Albrecht Ritschls Leben*, II, p. 49: 'Zu Weihnachten will ich hören, dass wir die *anthropoi eudokias* sind...Am Karfreitag will ich hören, dass wir die Gemeinde sind, die durch die vollbrachte Versöhnung gestiftet ist, zu Ostern, dass wir die Gemeinde sind, die Christus mit sich aus dem Tod geführt und mit sich in den Himmel gesetzt hat, um durch sie die Welt zu beherrschen...'

17. Smith to his father, 24 May 1869, Cambridge University Library ADD 7449 C116a.

18. Smith to his father, 12 August 1869, Cambridge University Library ADD 7449 C120a.

19. O. Ritschl, *Albrecht Ritschls Leben*, II, p. 101: 'Smith hätte am liebsten selbst das Buch übersetzt, und, da ihm dazu die Zeit fehlte, liess er es sich wenigstens nicht nehmen, die Übersetzung genau zu controliren'.

20. See above p. 66.

On 9 February 1877 Smith wrote as follows to Ritschl:

> Whether I come this year to Germany is extremely uncertain. How much more desirable it would be, if you could at least visit our home. I would take you around, dear Herr Professor, as the *Urvater* of the 'Aberdeen Heresy'.[21]

The phrase '*Urvater* of the Aberdeen Heresy' recurred more than once in their correspondence, although Ritschl himself did not quite know what to make of it, and we do not know whether Smith invented the phrase or, as seems more likely, took it up from one of his opponents.[22]

Bearing this in mind, when we turn to ask in what ways Ritschl influenced Smith, the question is not easy to answer. Ritschl was a New Testament scholar turned systematic and historial theologian. He did not, as far as I know, write or pronounce in an influential way on matters of Old Testament criticism. The nearest he came to discussing matters of interest to Smith was in the second volume of his great work on Justification, the subtitle of which was *Der biblische Stoff der Lehre*. This was first published in 1874 when, as I shall show in the next lecture, Smith's own critical views on the composition of the Pentateuch and the history of Israelite religion and sacrifice were well developed, as he kept abreast of the wider scholarly discussion in Germany and Holland. It is quite possible that Ritschl discussed with Smith the position that the 1874 volume would adopt; and in any case, Smith would almost certainly have read the 1874 volume when it appeared.[23]

Ritschl's main concern in this volume was to interpret New Testament material on the atonement in terms of the Old Testament; and in dealing

21. Smith to Ritschl, 9 February 1877 in O. Ritschl, *Albrecht Ritschls Leben*, II, p. 314. Smith's letter is given in German. Professor R. Smend informs me that none of the letters of Smith to Ritschl is extant, as far as he is aware.

22. Ritschl wrote to W. Mangold on 14 February 1877: 'Das [the title "Urvater der Aberdeen Heresy"] werde ich nun meinem Consistorialrath und dem andern Titelwesen hinzufügen; obgleich ich mich nicht entsinne, mit dem guten Manne jemals über die Pentateuchfrage gesprochen zu haben. Es ist sich nur offenbar auch anderer Heterodoxien bewusst, die ich in ihm erzeugt habe. Und wegen dieser werde ich ja zwar auch von den alten Weibern verläumdet, aber doch nicht verklagt.' See O. Ritschl, *Albrecht Ritschls Leben*, II, p. 314. Ritschl replied to Smith's letter of 9 February on 20 February 1877, Cambridge University Library ADD 7449 D605.

23. When I read the third edition of vol. II of Ritschl's *Die christliche Lehre von der Rechtfertigung und Versöhnung* (Bonn, 1889), in the Bodleian Library in 1978, the pages were uncut! In what follows, reference is to this edition. Vol. II was not translated into English.

with the Old Testament material Ritschl emphasized the covenant and played down the idea that individual offenders needed to propitiate God. In dealing with the levitical cult, Ritschl emphasized that it was a gracious ordinance of God which expressed and maintained the covenant relationship that he had established with his people.[24] God's punishment of the sins of individuals and the nation was not an expression of his anger but was a working out of the process whereby he was establishing justice among the covenant people, and ultimately in the whole world. God's guiding of this movement towards universal justice, concentrated in the first place through the covenant with Israel, was what distinguished the religion of Israel from that of her neighbours.[25]

Ritschl noted that there were differences in attitude towards sacrifice when the levitical cult was compared with what was found in the prophets and some of the Psalms. However, there is a tendency in Ritschl to play down this difference. The Psalms are seen within the context of the covenant. In the Psalms the faithful within Israel are those who are true to the covenant, while their enemies, whether Israelites or heathen, are opponents of the covenant. Where the Psalms speak of God's anger against those who are faithful, there is indeed a personal awareness of the righteousness of God. Yet the sense of estrangement that this brings is already overcome in the hope in God which his afflicted servants entertain.[26] The prophetic criticisms of sacrifice are not criticisms of the cult as such, but of a praxis that has subverted sacrifice from its place in the covenant and has put it at the service of a people who are indifferent to justice.[27]

This second volume of Ritschl's great work is a masterly piece of synthesis in the service of Ritschl's overall vision of God at work in history, establishing his kingdom of moral values, a kingdom that began in Israel and has received universal actualization and potential through Jesus. The most notable points of contact with Smith's work are, first, the insistence that God was specially at work in Israel in a way that was not true of Israel's neighbours, and secondly, the view of the three main traditions that we can call law, prophets and psalms as each in its way an aspect of God's gracious working in Israel. We can pick up other traces of Ritschlian influence also. For example, Smith's 1872 lecture on the

24. Ritschl, *Lehre von der Rechtfertigung*, II, p. 54.
25. *Lehre von der Rechtfertigung*, II, p. 95.
26. *Lehre von der Rechtfertigung*, II, pp. 130-38.
27. *Lehre von der Rechtfertigung*, II, p. 56.

critical study of the Psalter emphasizes the covenantal nature of the
Psalms. The following quotation gives the flavour of his position:

> The Psalter, as was to be expected from its character as a Theocratic
> poetry—a poetry of God's Kingdom and Church—is quite free from all
> that one-sided individualism and fanaticism by which many later hymns,
> however deeply they may express a real personal conviction, are rendered
> unfit to express the experience of the Church and of God's people at all
> times. The Psalms are in the fullest sense hymns of the Old Testament
> Church, sung that is by men whose sense of personal relation to God was
> always based on and rooted in their sense of God's redeeming relation to
> Israel.[28]

I shall point out, in my fifth lecture, that Ritschl's theology also had an
effect on Smith's sermons. Otherwise we can say that Ritschl enabled
Smith to gain the sense that, as a theologian working in the 1870s, he
was heir to a theological tradition that was not to be accepted uncriti-
cally, but was to be studied historically. Such study would be discrimi-
nating, identifying strengths and weaknesses, criticizing tendencies that
were less adequate understandings of Christianity, and emphasizing
tendencies that represented Christian theology at its best. The aim of this
historical study would be to articulate a theology for the present age,
and one representing the essence of Christianity. Being the sort of
person he was, it is likely that Smith would have wanted to be proficient
in historical and systematic theology. His many reviews, for example, in
the *British and Foreign Evangelical Review* dealt as frequently with
historical and systematic theology as with Old and New Testament
subjects. Ritschl, however, was the vehicle and focus by which Smith
found the type of theology with which he could identify and which, to
the best of my knowledge, he maintained to the end of his life. The
contac: with Ritschl also throws up another important fact, which is that
Smith, unusually among Old Testament scholars of the past century, did
his Old Testament study out of an interest in and acquaintance with
historical and systematic theology.

Smith's next important visit to Germany following that in 1869 was
in 1872, when he again went to Göttingen, in order to study Arabic with
Paul de Lagarde.[29] Lagarde (1827–1891) had had a difficult path to
academic preferment before he was appointed to succeed Heinrich

28. *Lectures and Essays of William Robertson Smith* (ed. J.S. Black and
G. Chrystal; London: A. & C. Black, 1912), p. 296.

29. Black and Chrystal, *Life of William Robertson Smith*, pp. 146-49.

Ewald in Göttingen in 1869.[30] Here, he devoted the remainder of his life to the textual criticism of the Greek version of the Old Testament, the completion of which, however, took second place to his work as a teacher. During his younger days he had had to do much teaching to earn his living, and this habit stayed with him. Alfred Rahlfs, who took over from Lagarde the work of producing a critical text of the Septuagint, related the story that, in the summer of 1885, Lagarde had arranged a lecture course on Syriac specially for Hermann Gunkel, and had arrived at the lecture theatre expecting to find only Gunkel there. On arrival he found that Rahlfs was also present and demanded to know what he was doing there![31]

In the light of this it is understandable that Smith was able to study Arabic with this great teacher on a daily private basis in the summer of 1872, and because of the great responsibility that Lagarde felt towards his former pupils, an acquaintance developed that endured for many years. This was in spite of the fact that Lagarde, who did not get on well with his colleagues, broke with Ritschl, and made his difference from his colleague clear in the following statement:

> I cannot understand how any doctrine of Justification and Atonement can be evangelical since, as any concordance under the entries *dikaioun* and *katallassein* shows, Justification and Atonement are never even mentioned in the four Gospels. These terms belong exclusively to Paul.[32]

Smith, then, maintained contact with this awkward man who sharply criticized the church and theology of his day, as well as the Jews. When Smith was applying for his first post in Arabic in Cambridge in 1882, Lagarde supplied a printed testimonial in English dated 1 December 1882 from which the following is an extract:

> Mr William Robertson Smith came over to Goettingen in the year 1872 in order to become my pupil in Arabic. As I was able to spend so much time on his behalf as to give daily private lessons to him, I consider myself fully

---

30. See R. Hanhart, 'Paul Anton de Lagarde und seine Kritik an der Theologie', in B. Moeller (ed.), *Theologie in Göttingen: Eine Vorlesungsreihe* (Göttinger Universitätsschriften Series A, 1; Göttingen: Vandenhoek & Ruprecht, 1987), pp. 271-305.

31. Cited in Hanhart, 'De Lagarde', p. 273.

32. Cited in Hanhart, 'De Lagarde', p. 291.

competent to bear witness to the uncommon energy with which he applied himself to his work, and to the brightness and clearness of intellect with which he mastered the most difficult parts of Arabic Grammar.[33]

The testimonial continues in detailing the progress that Smith made, and commends him to the electors for the post on the ground of his knowledge not only of classical Arabic, but his spoken knowledge of the language gained on trips to Egypt and Arabia. During his visits to the Orient, Smith had sought Lagarde's advice on what to do, and had sent letters from Arabia to Lagarde. Lagarde's acknowledgment of these contained typical unfriendly references to his colleague Ritschl:

> I have to thank you for your letters from Arabia, which will be carefully preserved, pasted upon paper. There is a good deal of very useful information in them.
>
> Lotze is probably going to Berlin. Ritschl's last book is horrid, in the worst style of his theology, and now he declares himself a Lutheran![34]

That Smith and Lagarde kept up a correspondence over many years in spite of obvious theological differences as well as violently differing opinions about Ritschl is an indication of the respect in which they held each other as scholars. The significance of Lagarde for Smith, in my view, was in convincing Smith of the importance of the textual criticism of the Old Testament based upon critical editions of the ancient Greek and Syriac versions. Smith became suspicious of the traditional Hebrew text of the Old Testament as a completely reliable witness to what the biblical authors wrote and, as I shall indicate in my third lecture, used this position to some effect in *The Old Testament in the Jewish Church*.

I am deliberately leaving to the end of this lecture an account of the German who, in my opinion, did most to shape Smith's theology so that he could combine evangelical faith with a full-hearted acceptance of biblical criticism. Before I come to him, I must mention briefly two further scholars, one of whom was Dutch and not German, with whom Smith maintained close contact, and who in their different ways shaped Smith's thought; I refer to Julius Wellhausen and Abraham Kuenen. These names will recur in lectures three and four; but some brief personal details will be in order here. For those who are interested, the

33. Cambridge University Library, ADD 7449 D379.

34. Black and Chrystal, *Life of William Robertson Smith*, p. 365. The letter is of May 1880. Lotze did move to Berlin, and died within weeks of his arrival. Ritschl's book is probably the first volume of his History of Pietism: *Geschichte des Pietismus*. I. *Der Pietismus der reformirten Kirche* (Bonn, 1880).

published proceedings of the Robertson Smith Congress will contain a comprehensive essay by Rudolf Smend on Smith and Wellhausen, while C. Houtmann has recently prepared an article on Smith and Kuenen.[35]

Smith first met Wellhausen probably in Göttingen in 1872, and their views on the history of Old Testament religion and literature converged over the next few years to the point where, in his 1881 lectures that became *The Old Testament in the Jewish Church*, Smith referred to Wellhausen's *Geschichte Israels* of 1878 as the most important book on the subject.[36] The two men grew closer together during the period of Smith's trials, and Wellhausen was one of the privileged persons on Smith's list, including Lagarde, of those to whom he sent information from Arabia.[37] After 1878, when he withdrew from his position in the theological faculty in Greifswald, Wellhausen had a difficult time academically and financially. Some of those difficultes are reflected in Wellhausen's letters to Smith. Thus, in June 1881 Wellhausen, who had an ill wife and a small salary, wrote saying that had things been better for him than they were, he would immediately have made a request for 3000 marks so that he could undertake a journey to Syria. This letter puts in a new light the criticisms of Wellhausen that were made by one of my distinguished teachers that he was an armchair scholar who never travelled to the Orient.[38] There is another sad letter from Wellhausen

35. Johnstone (ed.), *William Robertson Smith*. See also C. Houtman, 'William Robertson Smith (1846–1894): His Life and Work in the Light of his Correspondence with Abraham Kuenen', in J. Bremmer and H. Kippenberg (eds.), *The Rise of the Science of Religion in the Nineteenth Century: A Biographical Approach* (Supplements to *Numen*; Leiden: Brill, forthcoming).

36. See J.F. White, *Two Professors of Oriental Languages* (Aberdeen, 1899), p. 33, where he quotes a letter from Wellhausen, stating that 'I came to know Robertson Smith in 1871, when in our conversation he opposed my views with vigour'. The year was probably 1872, when Smith went to Göttingen to study Arabic. Wellhausen was still in Göttingen then, prior to his removal to Greifswald later the same year. For Smith on Wellhausen's *Geschichte*, see Chapter 6, pp. 99-100. However, Professor Smend has suggested to me that the date of meeting may have been 1869 and that the two men discussed Graf's recently-published views.

37. The list is given in a letter from Smith to J.S. Black written from Jeddah on 14 February 1880, Cambridge University Library ADD 7449 A70. The list includes W. Wright (Cambridge), T.K. Cheyne (Oxford), Dean Stanley, Prof. Briggs (Union Seminary), Lagarde (Göttingen), Hoffmann (Kiel), Wellhausen (Greifswald) and the 'old Delitzsch'. This list would be a useful reference point for trying to track down letters of Smith.

38. Wellhausen to Smith, 29 June 1883, Cambridge University Library ADD

from Marburg in October 1888: 'I have been badly treated in the world; Kautzsch, Nowack, Baudissin etc. have about three times as much salary and income as me...'[39] Interestingly, Smith did something to help Wellhausen's lack of income by commissioning well-paid articles from him for the *Encyclopaedia Britannica*.

Kuenen's role in Smith's development was two-edged. When Smith read Kuenen's *De godsdienst van Israël* (1869–70) he probably met for the first time the view of the history of Israelite religion that Wellhausen would present classically in 1878. There was probably an important influence here.[40] But Smith was also strongly repelled by what he called the Leiden School, and its insistence that Israelite religion contained no special revelation and was different from other Semitic religions in degree only and not in kind. As I shall argue in my third lecture, Smith's decision to study Arabic was a deliberate response to the Leiden School, Smith's intention being to master the sources for a knowledge of Semitic polytheism so that he could demonstrate the unique nature of Old Testament religion.

Kuenen drew close to Smith personally when, during the run up to his trials, Kuenen publicly rebutted the charge made against Smith that he was merely producing the ideas of Kuenen.[41] Correspondence led to deepening acquaintance, including a visit of Smith to Kuenen for a congress of Orietalists in Leiden. The interesting thing about Smith's contacts with men such as Wellhausen, Keunen and Lagarde was that he was able to agree with them in many aspects of biblical criticism while maintaining his own evangelical Christian convictions. That he was able to do this brings us to the most important aspect of Smith's German connection.

The theologian who influenced Smith most profoundly was Richard Rothe; yet Rothe died in August 1867. How, then, did Rothe influence Smith, and what is the evidence for this influence? We know from the memoir of Smith's father that, while he was in Bonn in the summer of

---

7449 D784: 'Wenn es mir besser ginge, würde ich alsbald um 3000 Mark für eine Reise nach Syrien bitten'.

39. Wellhausen to Smith, 23 October 1888, Cambridge University Library, ADD 7449 D811.

40. A. Kuenen, *De godsdienst van Israël tot den ondergang der Joodschen staat* (Haarlem, 1870), II, pp. 96-102 (trans. by A.H. May as *The Religion of Israel to the Fall of the Jewish State* [London, 1875], II, pp. 291-307).

41. See further Houtman, 'W.R. Smith'.

1867, Smith journeyed to Heidelberg to visit Rothe.[42] According to Pirie Smith, this was in July or August 1867, which means that Smith must have seen Rothe only weeks before the latter's death on 20 August 1867. That encounter must have made a great impression on Smith. Back in Edinburgh in March 1868 he wrote to inform his father that he had won an essay prize worth three guineas.

> I am going in wholly for German Books chiefly exegetical, Delitzsch on Isaiah, Keil's Minor Prophets, Rothe *Zur Dogmatik*, Hupfeld die Quellen der Genesis, Ewald's Grammar and for the rest probably Kamphausen's part of Bunsen's Bibelwerk…[43]

We note that, of the books to be obtained, the only one on systematic theology is Rothe's *Zur Dogmatik*. A few weeks later, on 1 June 1868, Smith was writing to his friend and later biographer J.S. Black who was teaching in Spain:

> Would you do me the favour to make some enquiries about Rothe. 1) If any brief biography has appeared since his death 2) if he has left behind him materials for a revised edition of the rest of his Ethics or Dogmatik and indeed anything you can gather about him. I am reading his books and would like to know something about him *personally*.[44]

In April 1869 when Smith left for his second visit to Germany, to Göttingen where he would hear Ritschl, we are told by Black who accompanied him that he was 'equipped with works on Mathematics and on Hebrew grammar and with Rothe's *Zur Dogmatik*'.[45] On 3 December 1869 he wrote to his father

> Last week I was taken up for a whole evening in writing an account of Rothe's Theory of church and State for Blackie. Blackie had given a quite false account of this…got from a very flimsy article by Gibb in the *Contemporary Review*.[46]

42. See Pirie Smith's *Memorandum*, Cambridge University Library ADD 7476 M, p. 40.

43. Smith to his father, 24 March 1868, Cambridge University Library ADD 7449 C94.

44. Smith to J.S. Black, 1 June 1868, Cambridge University Library ADD 7449 A1. A letter to Black dated 28 August 1868, 7449 A2, thanks Black for a pamphlet about Rothe.

45. Black and Chrystal, *Life of William Robertson Smith*, p. 111.

46. Smith to his father, 3 December 1869, Cambridge University Library ADD 7449 C127.

Smith's note was sent to the *Contemporary Review* but was not, as far as I can see, published. A lecture given by Smith to his fellow students in January 1869 on 'Christianity and the Supernatural' quoted Rothe, while, towards the end of his life, when asked to say which books had influenced him, he replied 'A.B. Davidson, Rothe (*Zur Dogmatik*), Ewald, Ritschl come into my mind at once as leading influences...'[47] We note the specific reference in the case of Rothe, and the general reference to the others. Readers of Smith's work who are on the look-out for references to Rothe will note comments such as the following in Smith's article in the *British Quarterly Review* for April 1879, 'On the Question of Prophecy in the Critical Schools of the Continent':

> The way in which believing critics, men who acknowledge not only the supernatural but the miraculous, deal with questions of date and authorship, is most instructively exemplified in Kamphausen's *Lied Mosis*. The arguments employed in that work are not the less interesting because the learned author is an admiring disciple of a man who left a strong personal mark on all his hearers—we refer to the late lamented Rothe.[48]

This reference to Kamphausen, incidentally, may explain why Smith visited Rothe from Bonn in July or August 1867. It is most likely that Kamphausen, with whom, as I indicated at the beginning of this lecture, Smith had conversations while in Bonn, suggested that Smith should visit his old teacher.

If I have overdone providing the evidence for Smith's interest in Rothe, and in particular for his *Zur Dogmatik*, this is because no one who has previously written about Smith's theological development has followed up the point in any detail. Other scholars do, of course, mention Rothe, and try to assess his influence. My impression, however, is that they have relied on secondary sources and have not tackled the 360 or so pages of German for themselves.

Richard Rothe, to whom I now turn, was born in Breslau in 1799 and was a student in Heidelberg from 1817–1819 where he was a member of the *Burschenschaft*, the politically active student association.[49] From 1819–1820 he studied in Berlin, where Hegel made a strong impression on him, and then from 1820–1823 he entered the theological seminary at Wittenberg. This seminary had been opened in 1817 following the

---

47. Black and Chrystal, *Life of William Robertson Smith*, p. 534.
48. Smith's *Lectures and Essays*, p. 182 n. 1.
49. For this and other details see A. Hausrath, *Richard Rothe und seine Freunde* (Berlin: Grote'sche Verlagsbuchhandlung, 1902–1906).

closing of the University of Wittenberg and its removal to and merger with the University of Halle.[50] It was intended to be a seminary where pietistic Lutherism would be taught to trainee clergy, in opposition to the 'rationalism' that was believed to infect universities such as Berlin and Halle. Indeed, the Wittenberg seminary was targetted by Berlin piestist circles for special attention and it was as a result of this activity that Rothe experienced a pietist conversion while at Wittenberg.[51] Thus for a time he belonged to the pietist movement and he later taught at the Wittenberg Seminary from 1828–1837.[52] In 1837 he took up a post in Heidelberg where, apart from a spell of four years in Bonn (where Ritschl was a young lecturer) from 1849–1853 he remained until his death in 1867.

As he grew older Rothe became increasingly unhappy with pietism. In his view, its opposition to rationalism led it to suspect all advances in human knowledge and to encourage superstition. Its churches withdrew from the wider world, and regarded it with suspicion. Its version of Christianity became increasingly remote from ordinary people. Its traditional doctrines such as the classical theological statements of the Trinity and the two natures in Christ were, in Rothe's view, a stumbling-block to faith.

Rothe found himself drawn strongly to the work of Bunsen, who saw in all the processes of history the guiding and educating hand of God, and for whom critical historical scholarship was not a threat, but a means of discovering the revelation of God in history. No doubt Rothe's youthful admiration for Hegel strengthened his openness to Bunsen's position; but Rothe also brought from pietism the opposite of what the pietists of his day were doing. They were stressing the importance of accepting traditional dogmas, whereas earlier in their history, their stress on religious experience led them to be indifferent to theological dogmas and religious institutions. Whereas the pietists were now wanting to make the churches a bastion against the advancing tides of modern knowledge, Rothe wanted to see in these advancing tides the guiding and educating hand of God. Thus, for Rothe, the task of theology was not to resist knowledge, but to mediate a personal experience of God that would

50.   See Rogerson, *W.M.L. de Wette*, pp. 147ff. See also O. Dibelius, *Das königliche Predigerseminar zu Wittenberg 1817–1917* (Berlin-Lichterfeld: Verlag von Edwin Runge, n.d).

51.   Dibelius, *Predigerseminar zu Wittenberg*, pp. 133-34.

52.   Dibelius, *Predigerseminar zu Wittenberg*, pp. 92-95.

enable knowledge to be seen as God-given. The result of this would be that the lives of ordinary people and every aspect of civil life would be drawn together in a national life that would be based upon knowledge of God and would be expressed in lives governed by ethical and moral responsibility. The church would no longer be an end in itself but a means to this greater, national religious goal. This, very roughly, is the view for which Rothe is best known in the history of theology, and which is usually given the label of *Kulturprotestantismus*—an amalgamation of Protestantism and national culture. The appeal of this side of Rothe's position to Smith would be in the belief that all advances in knowledge were an opportunity to see the guiding hand of God.

Rothe's *Zur Dogmatik*, which Smith studied so carefully, began life as three long articles in the *Theologische Studien und Kritiken* from 1855.[53] They were then revised, with account being taken of criticism, and appeared together in one volume in 1863. The first section, on dogmas, or formal doctrinal statements of churches, attacks the view that such statements are sacrosanct. If Christianity is understood as a community of believers brought into existence by the redemptive work of Christ, and if dogmas are defined as the attempt of Christian churches to articulate their understanding of what it means to know God through Jesus Christ, then it follows that dogmas are the work of people at particular times and places, and that they are not necessarily binding upon other, later believers. The Reformation was right to reject some of the dogmas of pre-Reformation Catholicism; however, it did not go far enough and should have rejected the Christology of Nicaea and Chalcedon. Dogmatics is a historical-critical enterprise, which should be based upon the Bible, modern knowledge and religious experience. If dogmas do not make sense of religious experience in the light of modern knowledge of the Bible and the world, then they are anachronistic impositions from past ages, puzzles that prevent rather than assist faith.[54] In a passionate conclusion to his first section Rothe argues that the greatest threat to Christian belief in his day comes not from the rejection by ordinary people of traditional dogmas, but from the strident assertion of these dogmas by orthodox churches. 'Whoever has the well-being of Christianity at heart must give up fear—fear not of unbelief, but of the truth and of critical investigation. Our dogmas are not God's word;

---

53. R. Rothe, *Zur Dogmatik* (Von Neuem durchgesehener und durchgängig vermehter Abdruck aus den Theol. Studien und Kritiken, Gotha, 1863).

54. Rothe, *Zur Dogmatik*, p. 51.

they are a human work, the work of scholars.'[55]

The second section, on revelation, is the shortest of the three. It emphasizes that God does not reveal information, but reveals himself in such a
way that he can be known at a personal level. How does he do this? By
the double action of manifestation and inspiration.[56] Manifestation is a
divine participation in human affairs that stirs the imagination, the
intellect or the emotions of people in such a way that they are inspired
thereby to see that they have encountered God. They are led to new
awarenesses of the divine purpose and will which they can then declare
to others. This means that the Bible is not God's revelation as such, but
is the *record* of how God's manifestation in the world has inspired new
understandings of him.

In the third, and by far the longest section, entitled 'Heilige Schrift'
(Scripture), Rothe attacks the 'old Protestant' view that the Bible is the
word of God. This led to the belief that the Bible was infallible, divinely
communicated information in the writing of which the biblical authors
played a passive role. Rothe is merciless in his account of the difficulties
that this belief produced: how belief in verbal inspiration ought logically
to entail the inspiration of the Hebrew vowel points; how it is hard to
maintain both that a text is verbally inspired by God and that it is
composed in poor Greek, as some of the New Testament is.[57] On this
part of the *Zur Dogmatik* Emanuel Hirsch wrote

> everything that can be said is presented so clearly and demonstrably that
> one wonders how any theologian could any more have the courage to
> repeat the old theory of inspiration.[58]

That is the negative side. What does Rothe say positively? The Bible's
authority derives from the fact that it was produced by people who were
inspired by the participation of God in human affairs to new awareness
of him. In the case of the New Testament, the divine participation was in
the life, death and resurrection of Jesus, and those who were inspired by

---

55. Rothe, *Zur Dogmatik*, p. 51: 'Wer es mit ihm [Christian belief] wohl meint,
muss vor Allem der Furcht den Abschied geben,—denn nicht der Glaube fürchtet
sich, sondern allein der Unglaube,—der Furcht für die Wahrheit und vor der
Kritik...Unsere Dogmen sind auch nach der ausdrücklichen Lehre unserer Kirche
nicht Gottes Wort, sondern menschliches Werk, Gelehrtenarbeit.'

56. Rothe, *Zur Dogmatik*, pp. 68ff.

57. Rothe, *Zur Dogmatik*, pp. 129-45.

58. E. Hirsch, *Geschichte der neuern evangelischen Theologie* (Gütersloh: Gerd
Mohn, 3rd edn, 1964), V, p. 404.

contact with him were his earliest followers, including Paul. This encounter produced the apostolic witness to Jesus which is at the heart of the New Testament. Yet those who encountered God in Christ and those who set down the apostolic witness in writing were not infallible people, even if they were inspired. This is why we have a *diversity of witness* to God's manfestation in Jesus in the New Testament. No one person's encounter could capture the whole truth or be free from error. It is when we put together the *varieties* of witness to Jesus that we begin to obtain a fuller picture of his significance—a fuller picture which the Holy Spirit working in human hearts can use to produce new encounters with God for readers in all generations.[59]

In the case of the Old Testament the equivalents of the apostles are the prophets. The prophets are those who are inspired by the divine participation in the events of Israel's history to see those events in their true light, and to see the God who is in and behind them; a God graciously guiding and teaching his people and leading them towards the redemption made fully possible by Christ.

This brief summary has hardly done credit to the book, nor have I mentioned the extensive footnotes in which Rothe not only took issue with his critics, but also enlisted as his allies on many points conservative theologians such as Tholuck and Kahnis, even though they would have rejected Rothe's overall position. In *Zur Dogmatik* Smith met an author of whose piety there could be no doubt. Time and again Rothe refers to the essence of religion as a personal awareness of God's graciousness. Rothe was totally committed to the Reformation, and saw the task of reformulating dogma and of redefining the role of the church in the light of modern knowledge as a continuation of what was begun at the Reformation. Yet this acceptance of modern knowledge was in no way a concession to rationalism. Rothe was an ardent supernaturalist; he believed that knowledge of God came only through a divine inititative, a divine participation in human history that inspired prophets and apostles in particular to see, understand and mediate this divine initiative.

In *Zur Dogmatik* Smith met a restatement of the doctrines of the inspiration and authority of the Bible that was welcoming to historical

59. Rothe, *Zur Dogmatik*, p. 286: 'die Verkündigung keines einzelnen Apostels ist schlechthin irrthumslos, aber die Gesammtverkündigung der Apostel (die apostolische Verkündigung in diesem Sinne) enthält vollständig die Bedingungen eines schlechthin irrthumslosen Verständnisses Christi. Und ganz dasselbe gilt auch von den Propheten und ihrer Verkündigung.'

criticism, and readily admitted that the Bible could contain errors, but which was essentially theologically driven and motivated, and insisted on the supernatural side of revelation. Rothe was stating how he believed the great reformers would have articulated the doctrine of Scripture had they lived in the nineteenth century; and Rothe's claim that the nineteenth century needed such a restatement of doctrine, and needed to be freed from the stranglehold of the Protestant orthodoxies of the seventeenth century, was throughout the book driven by the urgent pastoral and evangelistic need to communicate to his own geneneration the redemption that he had himself experienced in Jesus Christ.

The immediate impact made upon Smith by Rothe's *Zur Dogmatik* can be seen in the lecture given by him to his fellow students at the New College in January 1869 and entitled 'Christianity and the Supernatural'. It not only occasionally refers to Rothe; it is permeated with Rothe's ideas.[60] Smith argues that the Bible is not revelation, but the record of God making himself known to individuals and through history. He takes up the two key terms from the second section of *Zur Dogmatik*: manifestation and inspiration, which he calls the objective and subjective sides of revelation. He echoes Rothe's passiontate call for bringing the whole universe of thought under the lordship of Christ by means of a speculative theology 'in which the subjective consciouness of redemption is objectively evolved into a harmonious theory of the universe as reconciled to God in Christ'.[61]

So much for early and immediate influence; but how much of Rothe remained with him? In my view, Smith retained for the rest of his life Rothe's view of the inspiration and authority of the Bible. It enabled him to accept biblical criticism without reservation, and even to agree that there were errors in the Bible. But he was also able to affirm without reservation that the Bible was the record of a supernatural revelation and that it was the highest task of theology to investigate that revelation with a believing attitude and to present it to the world. As he said in his inaugural lecture in Aberdeen:

> We must let the Bible speak for itself. Our notions of the origin, the purpose, the character of the Scripture books must be drawn, not from vain traditions, but from a historical study of the books themselves. This

60. Smith, *Lectures and Essays*, pp. 109-36.
61. *Lectures and Essays*, p. 135.

process can be dangerous to faith only when it is begun without faith—
when we forget that the Bible history is no profane history, but the story of
God's saving self-manifestation.[62]

Other instances in which the influence of Rothe remained with Smith
were his emphasis on the importance of prophecy as forwarding the
knowledge of God, his conviction exemplified in his work for the
Encyclopaedia Britannica that new knowledge was to be encouraged
and brought into a view of the universe as redeemed by God through
Chirst, and the idea that no one apostle had the whole truth about
Christ, but that collectively their testimonies presented an adequate
picture. We find this latter view, I believe, in the ways in which Smith
described the three major sources of the Pentateuch in his article 'Bible',
three sources whose combinations of lay, prophetic and priestly insights
offered a picture of God's relationship with his people that no one
source could convey.

Smith's theology was forged in Germany because only German
theology (and Rothe's in particular) could offer an approach to the Bible
that saw biblical criticism as the necessary handmaid of a Christianity
that was deeply committed to a personal relationship with God through
Christ, and evangelistic in its wish to bring all knowledge under Christ's
lordship. That it led Smith to dismissal is no surprise; for today's church
in Britain is in some ways no nearer to appreciating this German type of
theology than was the church in Smith's day.

62. *Lectures and Essays*, p. 233.

Chapter 6

THE DEVELOPING CRITIC

William Robertson Smith lived and worked through the most exciting period in the modern history of biblical studies. When he was born in 1846 biblical studies was at what we might call an adolescent stage. The discipline was like a vigorous, but not entirely confident, older teenager, and one that was being kept somewhat in check by the combined efforts of parents and elders, by which I mean traditional, neo-orthodox and high church theology.[1] By the time of Smith's death in 1894 biblical criticism had come of age and was exercising an adult role in intellectual and theological life.

But we can narrow this down even more, and say that the period from 1867 to 1881, that is, from when Smith began his studies at the New College to when he was dismissed from the Aberdeen Free Church College, was the period when advances were made in Old Testament studies that have ever since marked a watershed.[2] Smith lived through these changes, he monitored their progress and he made a contribution to them. More than any other biblical scholar in Britain he was the man of the moment; and it is astonishing to remember that this 'man of the moment' was operating in a tiny classroom to under a score of students in the small and modest Free Church College, here in Aberdeen.[3]

The discovery that was made between 1867 and 1881 was that the developed levitical legislation attributed in the Old Testament to the founding work of Moses was in fact the creation of the post-exilic period; and that the prophets were the major creators of the distinctive faith of ancient Israel and not merely people who were referring back to Moses. A completely new picture of the history of Israelite religion and sacrifice emerged which saw it in terms of three main stages: an early

1.   See further my *Old Testament Criticism*, chs. 1–13.
2.   Rogerson, *Old Testament Criticism*, chs. 19–20.
3.   The room where Smith lectured, on the ground floor of the Free Church College (now Christ's College), cannot have held more than twenty students.

period from the time of the Judges to the ninth century, when Israelite religion was not dissimilar from that of its neighbours; the period beginning with the eighth-century prophets and ending with Josiah's reformation in 622 BCE when the great principles of ethical monotheism were proclaimed and legislated; and the post-exilic period when Israel's religion developed the levitical modes of holiness, priesthood and sacrifice. Some might object that the word 'discovery' for this new scholarly synthesis is misleading and claims too much.[4] Yet the synthesis has withstood many determined assaults upon it over the past century, and even if the word 'discovery' seems to have passed its sell-by date to our modern ears, it does not exaggerate the impact made upon biblical studies in Smith's lifetime. In this lecture I shall try to trace how Smith became convinced of the truth of the new synthesis, how he advocated it to the British public, and how his critical views on other aspects of the Old Testament developed as he grew older.

A fellow student, possibly the Revd B. Bell, in a reminiscence of Smith now in the Cambridge archive, mentions that Smith advocated the documentary theory of the composition of Genesis in a student essay written for A.B. Davidson in the session 1867–68.[5] At this particular moment in critical Old Testament scholarship there were two burning and interrelated questions.[6] Was the *Grundschrift* of the Pentateuch a unity, or were its laws and narratives to be assigned different dates? If it was a unity was it pre-exilic or post-exilic? In continental Europe this problem was being addressed by K.H. Graf, Abraham Kuenen and Theodor Nöldeke, while in the isolation of the British colony of Natal Bishop J.W. Colenso was making a British contribution to the matter.[7]

It appears that it was Kuenen who first suggested that the *Grundschrift* as a unity was post-exilic, although Graf was the first to publish this view in 1869 without acknowledging his indebtedness to Kuenen.[8] It was Colenso who had convinced Kuenen that the narratives of the *Grundschrift* must be late, even though Colenso himself still tentatively

---

4.   It must also be noted that much important work preceded the 1867–1881 period, notably that of scholars such as de Wette, Gramberg, George and Vatke. See Rogerson, *Old Testament Criticism*, chs. 2–4.

5.   Cambridge University Library, MS ADD 7476 M 10, pp. 3-4.

6.   Rogerson, *Old Testament Criticism*, pp. 259ff.

7.   Rogerson, *Old Testament Criticism*, ch. 16.

8.   See Kuenen's *De godsdienst van Israël*, II, pp. 96-102 (ET *The Religion of Israel*, II, pp. 291-307).

detached them from the legislation and dated them before the exile, when Part VI of his *The Pentateuch and Joshua* appeared in 1871. Smith took up his post as professor at the Free Church College in 1870, just at the point when these momentous ideas were beginning to take shape and to be firmed up. He almost certainly read Kuenen's presentation of the matter in an extended note to Kuenen's *De godsdienst van Israël* of 1869–70.

We get a glimpse of the fact that Smith was concerned with these questions from a review of the 1873 number of the Dutch periodical *Theologisch Tijdschrift* in the *British and Foreign Evangelical Review*.[9] Smith mentions a paper by W.H. Kosters which discusses the date of the historical or narrative portions of the Book of Origins, as Smith calls the *Grundschrift*, and notes that Kosters agrees with Kuenen. There then follow some of the few comments that we possess from Smith at this period on the general scholarship of this question:

> …As recent discussions have been much more busied with the legislative part of the book, and as Graf's original distinction between the Elohistic history and the Levitical Legislation is still upheld by Colenso, M. Kosters undertakes to vindicate at large the comparatively late character of the passages in question. Colenso's position scarcely calls for refutation and in fact has its origin simply in the fact that the Bishop, whatever new developments his views may undergo, never retracts his former statements. But the question of the relative age of the historical parts of the Pentateuch is one on which all new discussion is acceptable, even though, as in the present case, no new point of view is attained.[10]

This observation is intriguing and puzzling. It is not clear whether the criticism of Colenso is a criticism made by Kosters which Smith is retailing or whether it is Smith's own criticism. If it is the latter this would imply that Smith was inclining towards the unity of the *Grundschrift* if not a late dating. His comment that Kosters's discussion presents no new viewpoint conceals the epoch-making implication of dating the narratives along with the legislation as post-exilic. In all this, Smith may be acting prudently, and may be playing his cards close to his chest lest he cause alarm or provoke opposition. A review in the following volume of the *British and Foreign Evangelical Review* of the *Jahrbücher für deutsche Theologie* of 1873 mentions the inaugural

---

9.   W.R. Smith, 'German and Dutch Periodicals', *BFE* 22 (1873), pp. 376-84.
10.   Smith, 'German and Dutch Periodicals', p. 384.

lecture in Tübingen of the fairly conservative Old Testament scholar Ludwig Diestel.[11] Smith notes that although the approach is critical there is 'decided adherence to the old view of the place of the Elohist'.[12]

Smith presumably means the view that the *Grundschrift* as a unity is the oldest of the Pentateuchal sources; and it is interesting that he describes it as the 'old view', from which we might deduce that Smith favoured the 'new view' that was increasingly seeing the *Grundschrift* as the latest source. This view would be reinforced by notable books by August Kayser and Bernhard Duhm in 1874 and 1875 respectively.[13]

This brings us to the famous article 'Bible' in the ninth edition of the *Encylopaedia Britannica*, which Smith wrote in the summer of 1875 and which appeared at the end of 1875.[14] The article dealt with much more than the criticism of the Pentateuch. There were treatments of all parts of the Bible; and the section on the New Testament gave quite an airing, even though approval was denied, to the so-called Tübingen hypothesis of the composition of the Epistles and Gospels. However, in its presentation of the state of Pentateuchal studies and the implications of this for the history of Old Testament religion and literature, the article is astonishingly up to date. We must remind ourselves that it was only six or seven years earlier that the suggestion had first been made that the *Grundschrift* as a unity was post-exilic, and that by the time that Smith wrote the article this view was only beginning to receive scholarly reinforcement. Further, although Wellhausen was carrying out the researches that would be published as articles on the composition of the Hexateuch and his classic book on the history of Israel, none of these had yet appeared when Smith wrote the article 'Bible'.

In the article, Smith distinguished three main sources which ran through the Pentateuch and Joshua: a Levitico-Elohistic document (the *Grundschrift* or P); a Jehovistic narrative which, beginning with the creation, treated the early history 'more in the spirit of prophetic theology and idealism'; and a third author 'belonging to northern Israel, and specially interested in the ancestors of the northern tribes' (E). Smith associated these three sources with 'three currents of interest' that he believed determined the course of Israelite history: 'the traditional lore of

11. W.R. Smith, 'Dutch and German Periodicals', *BFE* 23 (1874), pp. 176-82.
12. Smith 'Dutch and German Periodicals', p. 182.
13. Rogerson, *Old Testament Criticism*, pp. 259-60.
14. Smith, 'Bible', pp. 634-48.

the priests, the teaching of the prophets, and the religious life of the more enlightened of the people'.[15] After the book of Joshua, the Levitico-Elohistic source disappeared, possibly leaving the other two sources to run on as far as the books of Kings. The whole history from Genesis to Kings had been edited by a Deuteronomic hand. Deuteronomy was dated to the seventh century.[16]

Smith left open the question whether the Levitico-Elohistic document was earlier or later than Deuteronomy. If it was later, then the system in which priests were superior to levites was the culmination of the development of the Israelite cult. If the Levitico-Elohistic document was *earlier* than Deuteronomy then its provision had existed as a legal programme long before the exile but the programme itself had not been fully carried out until after Ezra. As Smith hinted, 'the solution of this problem has issues of the greatest importance for the theology as well as for the literary history of the Old Testament'.[17]

We can forgive Smith for sitting on the fence. He was, after all, still not yet thirty, and the purpose of the *Encyclopaedia* article was to inform readers about the current state of research rather than to advocate a new theory which was still feeling its way. But he was clearly inclining to what would later be called the Wellhausen position. An article published in 1876 in the *British and Foreign Evangelical Review* is instructive here.[18] Entitled 'The Progress of Old Testament Studies', it was largely an attack on Pusey's commentary on the Minor Prophets; but, in favour of a progressive theology as opposed to the static theology exemplified by Pusey, Smith argued that the higher criticism placed 'the whole history of revelation before the manifestation of the Incarnate Word' in a new light. On the history of the Pentateuch and of Old Testament religion Smith wrote:

> the religious institutions of Israel had not really been stationary from the days of Moses. The Pentateuch itself embodies ordinances which belong to very different stages in the progress of law and worship; and the historical books confirm the truth that the institiutions of Judea after the captivity

15. Smith, 'Bible', p. 637.

16. Smith, 'Bible', p. 638.

17. Smith, 'Bible', p. 638.

18. W.R. Smith, 'The Progress of Old Testament Studies', *BFE* 25 (1876), pp. 471-93.

are not a mere literal revival of the laws of Moses, but the fruit of a long contest for purity of religion, in which each victory of spiritual religion over opposing forces was emobodied in a new development of the national ordinances.[19]

Smith went on to point out that if the laws concerning the centralization of worship at the Aaronic sanctuary had grown up gradually and reached their fullest development later rather than earlier, it became possible to understand how Samuel, Elijah and other great leaders had carried out their work in spite, on the traditional view, of being in breach of the Mosaic law. Further, the action of Ezekiel in sketching a new system of ritual ordinances for the temple after the restoration from exile became intelligible. On the old view, there was no need for Ezekiel's ordinances if those of Moses had already existed for centuries.

On this evidence, we can conclude that Smith had in effect adopted the Wellhausen position *before* he was able to read Wellhausen's literary and historical studies in the years 1876–1878. In fact, we have a brief notice of Wellhausen's analyses in the 1876 *Jahrbücher für deutsche Theology* in Smith's article 'The Study of the Old Testament in 1876' in the *British and Foreign Evangelical Review* for 1877.[20] The notice is but a long paragraph, concluding that Wellhausen's researches, even though incomplete, 'point to influences of great interest for the history of the Old Testament'.[21]

Further, Smith reviewed Wellhausen's *Geschichte Israels* in *The Academy* for 1879.[22] He made it clear that the book's importance lay not in its originality of ideas but rather in the manner in which the case had been put:

> The first section of the work investigates the history of the sanctuary, the sacrifices, the feasts, the priesthood, and the provision for the support of the clergy. Under each head an historical development is traced, beginning with observances of spontaneous and natural character, and advancing by stages corresponding to the development of the law from the Jehovistic ordinances of the Book of the Covenant through Deuteronomy to the priestly code. That this is the historical order of progress appears to be indisputable, and the main lines of evidence are not new. But Wellhausen

19. Smith, 'Progress', p. 491.
20. W.R. Smith, 'The Study of the Old Testament in 1876', *BEF* 26 (1877), pp. 779-805, reprinted in *Lectures and Essays*, pp. 367-99.
21. Smith, 'The Old Testament in 1876', *Lectures and Essays*, p. 382.
22. W.R. Smith, Review of Wellhausen's *Geschichte Israels* in *The Academy*, May 1879, reprinted in *Lectures and Essays*, pp. 601-607.

has strengthened them by many subtle and original observations, and has greatly increased the cumulative force of the argument by showing that it is possible to work the scattered data into a consistent and intelligible historical picture more complete than anything that has been hitherto attempted.[23]

In my opinion, no one has better stated than Smith in these words the importance and achievement of the *Geschichte Israels*; but these comments also help us to evaluate Smith's own development and achievement in this same field.

In the months of January to March in 1881, Smith gave a series of public lectures in Edinburgh and Glasgow that were published in May 1881 under the title *The Old Testament in the Jewish Church*.[24] The last five of these lectures were devoted to expounding the theory of Israelite religion and literature that has come to be associated epecially with the name of Wellhausen; and Smith's pupil and greatest disciple, Stanley A.Cook, described the lectures as 'the most original and, from the religious point of view, the most persuasive exposition and justification of the "Wellhausen hypothesis"'.[25]

But Cook wisely put the words 'Wellhausen hypothesis' in inverted commas. Whatever he may have intended by this (it may have been no more than a recognition that Wellhausen's contribution was primarily to give classical expression to work pioneered by a number of scholars including Wellhausen) we need to consider the matter further.

At one stage in my researches into Smith's critical development, I was inclined to assign more importance to Wellhausen's *Geschichte Israels* than perhaps was deserved. It was easy to see the *Geschichte* as helping Smith once and for all to make up his mind in favour of one of the two alternative positions that Smith had left in the balance in the article 'Bible'; and Smith did refer to the *Geschichte* in an endnote in *The Old Testament in the Jewish Church* as the most important book on the subject.[26] However, I am now inclined to see things slightly differently. I have tried to point out in this lecture how Smith's student and early teaching days coincided with the publications and researches that culminated in the *Geschichte Israels* and how his article on the progress of

23. Smith, Review of Wellhausen, in *Lectures and Essays*, pp. 602-603.

24. W.R. Smith, *The Old Testament in the Jewish Church: Twelve Lectures on Biblical Criticism* (Edinburgh, 1881).

25. S.A. Cook, *The 'Truth' of the Bible* (Cambridge: Heffer; London: SPCK; New York: Macmillan, 1938), p. 16.

26. Smith, *Old Testament in the Jewish Church*, p. 418.

Old Testament studies in 1876 more or less articulated the 'Wellhausen hypothesis' before Smith had even seen Wellhausen's literary researches. I am therefore now of the opinion that Smith had become convinced *before* the publication of the *Geschichte Israels* that the researches of Kuenen and others that were leading towards it, were likely to become the new established position, and that what finally persuaded him to go public on this was his conviction that Wellhausen had shown that it was 'possible to work the scattered data into a consistent and intelligible historical picture'.[27] Smith now believed that Wellhausen's reconstruction would convince critics of every school of the correctness of the position that he was championing.

All this must affect our estimate of Smith's last five lectures in *The Old Testament in the Jewish Church*. They are not a reworking of Wellhausen's *Geschichte Israels* into Smith's own way of thinking. Smith had been wrestling with these matters for many years, and had been considering how they could be put to the service of revealed religion. An important element in this was the place of prophecy, which is the subject of my fourth lecture. He was also already deeply interested in the question of how Israel's religion arose out of, yet differed fundamentally from, that of its neighbours. His lectures in *The Old Testament in the Jewish Church* were accordingly framed in a highly original manner.

Because I devoted an entire paper to *The Old Testament in the Jewish Church* at the William Robertson Smith Congress in April 1994 I shall give a much briefer resumé of lectures eight to twelve here.[28] The angle from which Smith approached the problem was that of the total religious experience of ordinary Israelites. The levitical ordinances as found in Exodus to Numbers present a complete theory of the religious life in which God is esssentially awesome and unapproachable. There is only one legitimate priesthood, and the ordinary Israelite can only approach Jehovah (Smith's preferred name for the God of Israel) via this priesthood at this sanctuary. Further, the whole of Israel is subject to laws of ritual purity whose breaching requires sacrifice to be offered at the single sanctuary, with the great ritual of the Day of Atonement covering any deficiencies of expiation.

According to the Old Testament itself, these ordinances were instituted by Moses and were therefore in place from the wilderness period

27. Smith, Review of Wellhausen, in *Lectures and Essays*, pp. 602-603.
28. For this lecture see Chapter 10 of the present book.

onwards. However, books such as Judges, Samuel and Kings present a quite different picture. Smith lists no fewer than fifteen sanctuaries that appear in these books as places where sacrifice is offered to God, or where he is worshipped. Yet, if the levitical legislation really had been in place since the time of Moses, these sancutaries were

> not simply less holy, places of less solemn tryst with Jehovah; they are places where His holiness is not revealed, and therefore are not, and cannot be, sanctuaries of Jehovah at all.[29]

Smith admits that one could explain this anomaly by assuming that the worship at these fifteen sanctuaries was heathen worship practised by apostasizing Israelites; the real difficulty is that some of these sanctuaries are connected with figures such as Samuel, who are presented in the Old Testament as faithful servants of God.

Smith concentrates upon the sanctuary at Shiloh, described in Jer. 7.12 as the place where God had set his name at first, and argues that if there was any sanctuary where the levitical legislation would be preserved and enacted, it would be Shiloh. Smith proceeds to show how the practices at Shiloh totally contradict the levitical legislation. His examples include the fact that Samuel ministered there even though he was not of a priestly family, that the ark of the covenant seems to have been visible to the public, and that the priests took by force the portions of meat to which they were entitled under the levitical legislation while they were condemned for doing this according to the customs at Shiloh. Smith observed that the ritual of the Day of Atonement could never have been carried out in the Shiloh temple. A section on prophecy enables Smith to contrast the awesome God of the levitical legislation with the tender and intimate images by which the prophets describe the relation between God and his people.

For his positive account of the religion and literature of the Old Testament Smith distinguishes three blocks of laws: what he calls the First Legislation (Exod. 21–23), the Deuteronomic Legislation (Deut. 12–26) and the Levitical Legislation. From each of these he reconstructs the social and religious life of the people. The First Legislation implies a society of landholders whose citizens are people of 'independent bearing and personal dignity' without a strong central authority, and where institutions such as blood revenge regulate murder and personal injury. The weekly sabbath and the sabbatical years help to prevent exploitation, and

---

29. Smith, *Old Testament in the Jewish Church*, p. 234.

they also provide for the poor and needy. Firstlings and first fruits are presented to God at the sanctuary, and a plurality of sanctuaries is implied. This type of society is what we meet with in Judges and 1 Samuel. Its legislation had much in common with the legislation of Israel's neighbours as did its worship. Nonetheless its belief in a national God Jehovah who had delivered his people from slavery in Egypt gave it a distinctive faith.

Unfortunately, this society could not avoid the tendency to degenerate into the heathenism of its neighbours, and this is what prompted the work of the prophets. They denounced heathen practices in Israel, and demanded a higher morality based upon a higher conception of the nature and purposes of God. But their preaching needed to be given legislative force, and this was what was done in the Deuteronomic Legislation. This legislation's insistence on a single sanctuary was aimed at preventing the assimilation of Israel's religion to that of its neighbours that came from their sharing sanctuaries. The Deuteronomic Legislation was the basis of Josiah's reformation in 622 BCE; but this was short lived, and after the exile a new approach was needed. Ezekiel's legislation for a restored temple was the impetus for priestly teaching to be gathered together and reformulated. The levites became inferior ministers, provision was made for regular offerings as part of the daily worship of God, and prominence was given to the sin offering and to atoning rituals. The process of formulating the Levitical Legislation lasted until the time of Ezra. As it concentrated more and more on the awesomeness of God and on restricted access to him for ordinary worshippers, so there developed new forms of spiritual, non-ritual religion, in the tradition of the prophets and as expressed in the Psalms. The setting for this non-ritual religion was the synagogue.

In the Levitical Legislation the religion of Israel had reached the end of a long development which, in spite of the restricted access to God for ordinary Israelites that it entailed, preseved the spirit of Israelite religion. As Smith remarked:

> The legal ritual did not satisfy the highest spiritual needs, but it practically extinguished idolatry. It gave palpable expression to the spiritual nature of Jehovah, and, around and within the ritual, prophetic truths gained a hold of Israel such as they never had before.[30]

So far, I have dealt with Smith as the developing critic in the area that was the most crucial in the scholarship of his day. I now turn to trace his

---

30. Smith, *Old Testament in the Jewish Church*, pp. 313-14.

development in other areas. Smith's friend John F. White records a letter written to him by Wellhausen which begins as follows:

> I came to know Robertson Smith in 1871, when in our conversation he opposed my views with vigour. Afterwards we had much correspondence.[31]

This letter raises two questions, the date of the meeting and the content of their discussion. The most likely date is 1872, when Smith was in Göttingen studying Arabic with Paul de Lagarde.[32] What did they discuss? In 1872 Wellhausen's main publication was on the text of the books of Samuel, which was intended as preparatory work for a new critical edition of the Hebrew Bible.[33] It made considerable and daring use of the Greek version of the Old Testament for recontructing the original Hebrew text. It is not impossible that this is one of the matters they discussed. In his lecture on the Progress of Old Testament Studies published in 1876 Smith referred to Wellhausen's textual criticism of the books of Samuel in a qualified manner.[34] Further, he spoke with approval of the work of Lagarde, who had worked out a scheme for studying the textual transmission of the Greek version as a preliminary to producing a critical edition of the Septuagint, which would then assist the textual criticism of the Hebrew Bible. It is not unlikely that Lagarde had spoken to Smith critically about Wellhausen's use of what Lagarde regarded as an uncritical Greek text for correcting corruptions in the Hebrew, and that this is what Smith and Wellhausen discussed. It is, of course, possible that they discussed what would later be called the Wellhausen hypothesis. Whatever the truth about this, Smith's interest in textual criticism played an important role in his development as a critic.

In the lecture on the prospects for Old Testament studies just referred to, Smith strongly critizised Pusey for basing his commentary on the Minor Prophets on the Authorized Version. This begged many questions, among them the reliability of the traditional Hebrew text. After long discussion of this, Smith declared

---

31. J.F. White, *Two Professors of Oriental Languages* (Aberdeen, 1899), p. 33.

32. Black and Chrystal, *Life of William Robertson Smith*, pp. 148ff. See also my comments in Chapter 5 n. 36 p. 84.

33. J. Wellhausen, *Der Text der Bücher Samuelis untersucht* (Göttingen, 1872).

34. Smith, 'Progress', p. 484: 'whatever defects are to be found in a work like Wellhausen's textual criticism of the Books of Samuel, the advance in accuracy of method and certainty of results over last century is palpable'.

it is certain, that there was no standard text even in Palestine till at any rate
about the time of Christ, and there is a very high probability, that the received
text is derived from a single archetype, and perpetuates all its faults.[35]

The implications of this were not only that the traditional Hebrew text
diverged from the text held by traditional believers to be inspired (that
is, the autograph), but that there was not much likelihood that the text of
these autographs could ever be completely recovered. But Smith had
important capital to make from this. In his article the following year on
Old Testament studies he reviewed a pamphlet by Hollenberg on the
difference between the Hebrew and Greek versions of Joshua. He
pointed out the evidence that this provided that Hebrew scribes copied
their manuscripts with such freedom that the traditional Hebrew text
contained large additions that were missing from the Hebrew texts that
lay before the Greek translators. 'Facts like these', wrote Smith,

> must be kept in view by every one who wishes to understand the gradual
> process by which the historical books of the Old Testament came to be the
> complex structure which they are.[36]

Smith's point, which was to be developed in *The Old Testament in the
Jewish Church*, was that there was little difference in the ancient world
between scribes and authors. Just as scribes were happy to add material
to the manuscrupts they were copying so authors worked by adding one
account of an event to another. Thus textual criticism was not simply a
matter of discovering *what* the biblical authors wrote. It provided crucial
evidence for *how* they wrote.

In *The Old Testament in the Jewish Church* Smith used this insight in
one example which still greatly worries students today, as I know
because I have deliberately used Smith's material. Smith printed out Jer.
27.1-22 (which is Jer. 34.5-22 in the Septuagint) in such a way as to
indicate that the Hebrew text was longer than the Greek. Material
common to both is in Roman type, while the material that is additional
and only in the Hebrew is printed in italics.[37] The surprising point that
emerges is that in the Greek version there is a prophecy that the vessels
of the temple will be taken to Babylon but it says nothing about them
being returned, while the Hebrew version declares that they will be
brought back. Smith concludes:

---

35. Smith, 'Progress', p. 485.
36. Smith, 'The Old Testament in 1876', *Lectures and Essays*, pp. 370-71.
37. *Old Testament in the Jewish Church*, pp. 113-14.

this is plainly the spurious insertion of a thoughtless copyist...That such a
prediction now stands in the text only proves what the thoughtlessness of
copyists was capable of, and makes the reading of the Septuagint
absolutely certain.[38]

This enabled Smith to conclude that Jeremiah never prophesied the
return of the temple vessels, thereby removing what would have been
an inconsistency in his teaching. But there was an implication here that
has never been followed up, and which can still worry students: the
traditional Hebrew text on which all our church authorized translations
of the Bible are based is sometimes quite misleading about what
prophets actually prophesied!

I turn to a quite different question, which was a favourite topic of
Smith, and where we can see considerable changes in his position: I
mean the study of the Psalms. If we can trust Smith's sermons to
indicate his critical views, then he seems to have held very traditional
views about some psalms when he began to teach at the Free Church
College. He appears to have accepted that Psalm 90 was a psalm of
Moses, and that Psalm 32 was by David;[39] that is, he accepted the
evidence of the titles of these psalms. By the time he gave the lectures
that became *The Old Testament in the Jewish Church* his views had
become much more radical. He divided up the five books of psalms into
three main collections. The first collection coincides mostly with the
traditional Book I of the Psalter, that is, Psalms 3–41, the first Davidic
collection. The second collection is found in Books II and III (Pss. 42–89)
where, however, they must be rearranged into a second group of Davidic
psalms and what Smith calls the Levitical Hymns or Psalms, that is,
those assigned in the titles to the levitical musical guilds, the sons of
Asaph and Korah. The third collection is Books IV and V (Pss. 90–150).

Smith discusses the collections in reverse order. The third collection,
Books IV and V, is clearly liturgical in character and designed for the
temple service. It must be later than the time of Ezra and Nehemiah,
who provided specially for the music of the temple. On the two collections of Levitical Psalms, Smith is cautious. Psalms 74 and 79 mention

38. *Old Testament in the Jewish Church*, p. 116.

39. On Psalm 32 see the sermon prepared in Göttingen in July 1872, Cambridge
University Library ADD 7476 K4. There are two undated, but presumably early
sermons on Psalm 90 in which it is asserted that the Psalm was a prayer of Moses, or
at least reflected his thoughts towards the end of forty years in the the wilderness. See
ADD 7476 K7 and K8 (which is stated wrongly in the catalogue to be on Eccl. 4).

the destruction and defilement of the temple, while other psalms protest the absolute loyalty of the psalmist in never having worshipped other gods, and complain about religious persecution. These considerations indicate a post-exilic date, but raise questions about references to the defilement of the temple. Smith mentions that the Persian general Bagoses defiled the temple in the reign of Artaxerxes II (404–359) and says that the psalms cannot be earlier than this. He also mentions, without naming it explicitly, the Maccabean theory, which would date these psalms to the desecration of the temple by Antiochus IV in 167 BCE. But Smith remains cautious: 'This conclusion, indeed, is refused by many scholars, and I do not put it forth categorically'.[40] On the other hand, Smith allows that some of the Korahite psalms, for instance Psalm 45, must be earlier than the exile.

Dealing with the two Davidic collections, Smith advances reasons against their being by David; for example, that David could not refer to the temple because it had not yet been built. He concludes that the first collection belongs 'to the early ages of Hebrew psalmody from David downwards'[41] without necessarily containing any psalms by David, the collection as a whole dating from the Babylonian exile. Smith does not date the second Davidic collection, but readers must infer that it is later than the first.

In 1892 Smith issued a revised and enlarged edition of *The Old Testament in the Jewish Church*, and it is interesting to note that one of the most substantially rewritten lectures was that on the Psalms.[42] In the eleven years since the first edition, Smith's dating of the Psalms had become even more radical. In the new edition Smith began his dating exercise with the Levitical Psalms of Asaph and Korah and although he still inclined to date them in the period 430–330 he was much more ready to acknowledge openly that the time of Antiochus IV was a possible reference point for some of the psalms. His point in the first edition that this was refused by many scholars was replaced by the observation that it was accepted by 'many of the best modern writers

40. *Old Testament in the Jewish Church*, p. 197.

41. *Old Testament in the Jewish Church*, p. 202.

42. W.R. Smith, *The Old Testament in the Jewish Church: A Course of Lectures on Biblical Criticism* (2nd edn, London, 1892). In the new edition the number of lectures is increased to thirteen, the end notes of the first edition become footnotes, and there are additional notes at the end of the book. See pp. 188-225 for the revised treatment of the Psalms.

on the Psalter'. However, Smith declared that he felt a difficulty 'in admitting that any of these pieces is later than the Persian period'.[43]

Perhaps the reason for this was that Smith now came out strongly in favour of a Maccabean dating for many of Psalms 90–150, and that to put the Levitical Psalms in this same period would upset what Smith thought to be the sequence of the three collections. Some of the psalms in 90–150 were assigned by Smith to the period of Ptolemaic rule (c. 330–200) when Israel enjoyed peace and prosperity; but others such as Psalm 149 expressed the militant piety of the Jews who had defeated Antiochus and had rededicated the temple in 165–164. Indeed, Smith assigned Psalms 113–118, the *hallel* psalms, to the rededication of the temple after the Maccabean victory. The collection of Psalms 90–150 and thus of the Psalter as a whole was dated to the early years of Maccabean sovereignty.[44]

Smith reserved his most radical alteration of viewpoint for the first Davidic collection. In 1881 he saw these psalms as coming from the time of David onwards. In 1892 he had become convinced that this collection formed the oldest part of the temple liturgy; but which liturgy and for which temple? Because he could find no evidence in the Old Testament historical books of organized worship or of guilds of singers during the time of the first temple, Smith concluded that

> even Book I of the Psalter did not exist during the Exile, when the editing of the historical books was completed, and that in psalmody as in other matters the ritual of the second Temple was completely reconstructed.[45]

As to the date of Book I, its adoption for a regular service with a formal liturgy was most likely at the time of Nehemiah. These psalms, full of spiritual elements, were 'the necessary complement of the law as published by Ezra'.[46] The second Davidic collection was decidedly later than the time of Nehemiah.

The 1892 edition of *The Old Testament in the Jewish Church* put the Psalms into a comparatively narrow time span, from around 440 to 150 BCE. This was a far cry from twenty years earlier when Smith apparently accepted Psalm 90 as Mosaic and Psalm 32 as Davidic! Yet it cannot be emphasized too strongly that these changes in his critical

43. *Old Testament in the Jewish Church*, 2nd edn, p. 207.
44. *Old Testament in the Jewish Church*, 2nd edn, p. 212.
45. *Old Testament in the Jewish Church*, 2nd edn, p. 219.
46. *Old Testament in the Jewish Church*, 2nd edn, p. 221.

views were not the result of changes in his religious opinions, as though a growing religious scepticism, a drawing closer to the position of, say, Kuenen, made him more ready to accept radical critical positions that he would have rejected when he was younger and had more faith. That he became more willing to accept positions that earlier he would have rejected is obvious from what I have said about his views on the Psalms. But his willingness to be more radical was a result of his conviction, fully formed by at least 1874 and going back to his study of Rothe, that believing criticism was essential for the maintenance and spread of evangelical Christianity; that historical criticism was not a threat to faith but something without which faith would become a puzzle to thinking people.

Smith addressed this matter in various places, especially from 1876 onwards; but nowhere did he address it better than in his account of Old Testament studies published in 1876, in which he implicitly cast Pusey in the role of those who opposed him in the Free Church.[47] Over against what he called Pusey's 'stationary theology', a theology whose only task was to expound a deposit of teaching vouchsafed to the church long ago and which could not be altered except to its detriment, Smith opposed a developmental theology concordant with the needs of each age. Smith cited Lessing's view that a constant impulse to new inquiry was a better gift of God to humanity than 'the immediate possession of all truth without a struggle, and without the possibility of error'. Addressing himself to the paradox that, while we possess truth we must also always be in search of the truth, Smith wrote:

> truth, like all moral and spiritual good things, is of worth only in so far as it is reached by pursuit and toilsome effort. The truths of revelation can form no exception to this law; for they too are meant to act on man, not magically, but morally. Hence it was that God unfolded his plan of salvation by slow degrees and not to the careless ear of men who had known no spiritual struggle, but to the longing souls of prophets and psalmists in their deepest conflicts with ungodliness and unbelief, when they looked to him and were lightened, and their faces were not ashamed. And so even now the full manifestation of God in Jesus Christ does not dispense either the individual believer or the church from constant search after a fuller understanding of God's truth...If it is true of the experimental life of the believer, that a saving apprehension and possession of Christ is only to be

47. 'Progress', pp. 471-93.

found in a constant and prayerful seeking after Christ to find him anew in every new need; it is not less true that a right apprehension of theological truth is inseparable from a constant and earnest search after new truth.[48]

The closing words of this quotation sum up Smith the developing critic. His move to more radical positions was part of this earnest search after new truth, and was driven by his belief that what he was investigating was the history of God's revelation, and that what he was discovering was an ever truer account of the history of grace.

This brings me to the last point of this lecture. Why did Smith decide to go to Göttingen in 1872 to study Arabic? As far as I am aware, we do not possess any explicit information from Smith about why he made this move; but it is possible, I believe, to make a conjecture. In his review of Old Testament studies for 1876 Smith designated what he regarded as 'the burning questions of the moment'. 'What is the origin and history of the spiritual monotheism of the prophets? How does it stand related to the conception of Jehovah among the mass? What is the relation of Jehovah to heathen gods, and of the worship of Jehovah in Israel to other worships?'[49]

One answer to these questions had been given by Kuenen and the Dutch school, and this was that there was 'no specific difference between the development of the Old Testament religion and that of other faiths'. This answer did not satisfy Smith, who saw its approach as subverting theology from being the study of God to being the study of religion. At the same time, Smith agreed that the Dutch theory had been upheld ably. If it was to be refuted, if, to quote Smith again,

the new science of comparative religion has laid upon biblical scholars the duty of examining more precisely the relation of the Hebrew faith to Semitic polytheism,[50]

this was a task which Smith was not prepared to leave to others, and which was almost certainly behind his decision to master Arabic so as to work out this question himself. This may help us to answer another question. What would have happened if Smith had not been dismissed from Aberdeen in 1881, but had continued as an Old Testament professor instead of becoming a professor of Arabic at Cambridge? It is tempting to see the move to Arabic as a move away from biblical

48. 'Progress', pp. 475-76.
49. 'The Old Testament in 1876', *Lectures and Essays*, pp. 391-92.
50. 'The Old Testament in 1876', *Lectures and Essays*, p. 391.

studies, a move towards a more secular career now that his church had deemed him unfit to be one of its theological teachers. To conclude thus would be to conclude wrongly, in my view. No doubt the Aberdeen dismissal and its immediate aftermath caused a diversion, but it did not alter the main course of Smith's career. We must not suppose that, had Smith remained in Aberdeen, he would have written about Old Testament subjects rather than about Arabian studies. Indeed, his article 'Animal Worship and Animal Tribes among the Arabs and in the Old Testament' which appeared in July 1880 and helped to bring about his dismissal is an Aberdeen piece of research involving Arabian studies.[51]

It was thus entirely appropriate that it was in Aberdeen that Smith gave the lectures that became famous as *The Religion of the Semites*. These lectures were not only the high point of Smith's researches into Arabian and Semitic heathenism (as he called it); they were intended to vindicate his belief, expressed in the last series of Burnett lectures, that only a divine revelation could have enabled Hebrew religion to emerge from the Semitic polytheism in which it was cradled.[52] The prophets, who played a crucial part in this process, are the subject of my next lecture.

51. W.R. Smith, 'Animal Worship and Animal Tribes among the Arabs and in the Old Testament', *Journal of Philology* 19 (1880), pp. 75-100; reprinted in *Lectures and Essays*, pp. 455-83.
52. See below, pp. 145-47.

Chapter 7

THE IMPORTANCE OF PROPHECY

Old Testament prophecy was a subject that fascintated Robertson Smith throughout his life. His lecture notes from his student days in Edinburgh record the reading that he was doing for an essay on the connection of prophecy with history—a reading list that included several titles in German—while he returned to the theme of prophecy towards the end of his life in the Fourth Lecture of the Third Series of Burnett Lectures.[1] In between, Smith published a book entitled *The Prophets of Israel and their Place in History* (1882) and during the 1870s gave courses of lectures on prophecy, some of which were published posthumously.[2]

Prophecy occupied an important position in the traditional apologetic of Protestantism, and it came to occupy an important position in Smith's understanding and defence of Christianity. Needless to say, Smith's position differed significantly from the traditional view.

According to that traditional view, prophecy secured at least three things. First, it proved that the Bible was a supernatural revelation from God. It did this because the prophets were held to have forecast events hundreds of years before they happened. Thus Isa. 7.14 predicted the Virgin Birth of Jesus and Isa. 52.13—53.12 predicted his atoning death and resurrection. The prophets could only have made such predictions

1.   For the lecture notes see Cambridge University Library ADD 7476 J7 pp. 7ff. For the essay reading see p. 40. The German titles include the last volume of E.W. Hengstenberg's *Christologie des Alten Testaments* and F.A.G. Tholuck's *Die Propheten und ihre Weissagungen*. Also, F. Delitzsch is mentioned in connection with Isa. 40–66. These are all comparatively conservative works. This is a general mention of Knobel and Hitzig but no reference to specific books. For the Burnett Lectures see ADD 7476 esp. H13 and H16.

2.   W.R. Smith, *The Prophets of Israel and their Place in History to the Close of the Eighth Century BC* (Edinburgh, 1882). A new edition was published by A. & C. Black, London, in 1919. Smith's text is unaltered but there are notes and an introduction by T.K. Cheyne.

with supernatural help. Secondly, because the Bible was supernaturally assisted, it was inspired and therefore true. Thirdly, the pattern of prophecy and fulfilment, which was strongly attested in the New Testament, provided an agenda for interpreting the Old Testament. The latter consisted of a series of prophecies of the coming of Jesus and, in its institutions and great leaders, a number of types pointing to Christ and to the institutions of the New Covenant.

There was also another point fundamental to the traditional interpretation of prophecy: the belief that some, perhaps many, prophecies had yet to be fulfilled or had only recently been fulfilled. Thus we find even such a scholarly and level-headed commentator as Dr Adam Clarke in 1825 interpreting 'the abomination that maketh desolate' in Dan. 12.11 in terms of the establishment of Islam, and the turning of the Church of St Sophia into a mosque. In that case, the abomination would be removed in 1290 days, i.e. years, which meant that in 1902 (1290 years after 612) 'the religion of the False Prophet will cease to prevail in the world'.[3] It is also the case that the French revolution and its aftermath made many believe that the end of papal power was in sight and that a new age was imminent.[4] In the late 1820s five conferences were held at Albury in the south of England under the patronage of Henry Drummond, whose aim was to determine which prophecies had been fulfilled in the life of Christ and in the history of the Christian church so that the prophecies waiting to be fulfilled could be identified.[5] The sense that people were living in the 'last times' was sufficiently strong for there to be renewed interest in evangelizing the Jews and in promoting the return of the Jews to Palestine. Further, the sense of an imminent new age was informed in some circles by the outbreak of 'Pentecostal' phenomena such as speaking in tongues. Port Glasgow was the scene of one such outbreak;[6] and although we must not push too far the point that I am about to make, Edward Irving, whose church in London

3.   A. Clarke, *The Holy Bible with a Commentary and Critical Notes*, V (London, 1825), on Daniel 12.

4.   See R.E. Clements, 'George Stanley Faber (1773–1854) as Biblical Interpreter', in P. Mommer and W. Thiel (eds.). *Altes Testament, Forschung und Wirkung: Festschrift für Henning Graf Reventlow* (Frankfurt: Peter Lang, 1994), pp. 247-68.

5.   On the Albury conferences see C.G. Flegg, *'Gathered under Apostles': A Study of the Catholic Apostolic Church* (Oxford: Clarendon Press, 1992), pp. 34ff. A list of the participants is given on pp. 37-38.

6.   Flegg, *'Gathered under Apostles'*, p. 42.

became the scene for Pentecostal phenomena in the 1830s after his removal from Scotland, had at one time served as assistant to Thomas Chalmers, the principle leader of the 1843 Disruption.[7]

In Germany, things were quite different. Beginning in the late eighteenth century a critical approach to the prophetic literature had begun to be built up which began to question whether everything ascribed to a prophet was authentic, and this had laid the ground for the interpretation of the prophets within their historical contexts. Notable commentaries by Gesenius on Isaiah (1820–21) and Hitzig on the Twelve Minor Prophets (1838), Jeremiah (1841) and Ezekiel (1847) were the forerunners of modern critical commentaries, and notable work was that by Heinrich Ewald in the form of a three-volume treatment of all the Old Testament prophets, which appeared in 1840–41.[8]

However, this German critical work was not unopposed in Germany. At the same time that there were Pentecostal outbreaks in Britain there was a resurgence of Protestant orthodoxy in Germany, associated with men such Hengstenberg, Keil and Delitzsch.[9] One of the results of their work was to impose a doctrinal agenda on the interpretation of the Old Testament, and to accuse anyone who interpreted prophecies such as Isa. 7.14 historically rather than as predicting the Virgin Birth of being a rationalist or of denying that prophets had divine assistance. The same charge was brought against anyone who argued that a part of Isaiah was not spoken or written by the eighth-century prophet of that name. An interesting mediating position was taken in Germany by von Hofmann. He interpreted Old Testament prophecies historically, but believed that Old Testament history as a whole was prophetic; that is, each generation of prophets spoke to their contemporaries about God's will, thus preparing the way for the next generation. Old Testament history was thus a succession of stages, each leading to the next, until the fulfilment was reached in Christ.

When Smith began his studies at New College, Edinburgh in 1866 he was fortunate to be taught by a man who combined a sober criticism with deep Christian faith, and who gave Smith the best possible foundation for the study of prophecy. That man was the reticent A.B. Davidson, who had himself studied in Göttingen and who had become a moderate

---

7.   See Flegg, '*Gathered under Apostles*', pp. 46-47 for a brief acount of the Pentecostal phenomena at Irving's London church.

8.   See generally, Rogerson, *Old Testament Criticism*.

9.   Rogerson, *Old Testament Criticism*, chs. 5 and 7.

disciple of Ewald's approach to prophecy.[10] However, to judge from Smith's lectures notes, Davidson's lectures were far from being one-sided. The key definition of prophecy that we find in Smith's notes—'So far as Hebrew usage goes the word is not mere speaker but one who speaks for another'[11]—is straight out of Ewald, a second edition of whose *Propheten des Alten Bundes* had just been published.[12] But Davidson had also referred to conservative German scholars such as Hengstenberg and Tholuck, and when Smith notes the reading that he was to do for his essay on prophecy and history, the list includes conservative scholars such as Hengstenberg, McCaul, Tholuck and Delitzsch.[13]

Incidentally, we may infer from Smith's lecture notes that his teacher had not fully understood Ewald's position. There is an entry that seems to indicate that Davidson disagreed with the view of Ewald that revelation is the work of the human heart.[14] In an article on prophecy published by Smith in the *British Quarterly Review* for April 1870, he specifically mentioned that Ewald had been described as holding that there was no specific difference between Hebrew and heathen prophecy. While Smith allowed that there might be some expressions of Ewald that might lead to that conclusion, he himself denied the allegation: 'Ewald does not hesitate to speak of the spiritual religion of Israel as standing in direct antithesis to heathenism as *the true religion*'.[15]

In his approach to prophecy, Smith had been encouraged by his teacher and by his reading to start from the historical setting of the prophets and the messages that they were delivering to their contemporaries. This was work that could be done by any scholar with the necessary

10. See J. Strahan, *Andrew Bruce Davidson* (London: Hodder & Stoughton, 1917).

11. Cambridge University Library ADD 7476 J7, p. 13.

12. H. Ewald, *Die Propheten des Alten Bundes* (Göttingen, 1866), I, p. 6: 'Ein Prophet ist nach seinem ursprünglichen Begriffe nicht Prophet für sich sondern für andere Menschen'.

13. See n. 1. For further information on Hengstenberg, Tholuck and Delitzsch see Rogerson, *Old Testament Criticism*. A. McCaul (1799–1863) was a missionary to the Jews before becoming Professor of Hebrew at King's College, London.

14. Cambridge University Library ADD 7476 J7, p. 13.

15. W.R. Smith, 'Prophecy in the Critical Schools of the Continent', *BQR* (April 1870). Reference is made in the present lecture to the republished version, 'On the Question of Prophecy in the Critical Schools of the Continent', in *Lectures and Essays*, p. 190.

training and linguistic equipment. But it raised a prior question of great importance that was bound to affect how the task of interpreting individual prophets was understood. Basically, the question was this: were the prophets of Israel inspired by God; or were they inspired men like inspired men of other religions? If they were inspired by God, then there was somewhere a divine revelation in their words, and what they proclaimed about the involvement of God in the historical events of their nation was in some sense true. This in turn affected how readers viewed the history of Israel. It was not just any history, but a history being guided and directed by God. If the prophets of Israel were merely inspired men like inspired men of other religions, then there was nothing special about the history of Israel. The teachings of the prophets could be admired for their high moral ideals and their concern for social justice; but they represented nothing more than a high achievement of sensitive and imaginative human beings.

The view that the prophets of Israel were no different in kind from other prophets of the ancient world had been argued by the great Dutch scholar Abraham Kuenen in the second volume of his *Historisch-kritisch onderzoek* of 1863, which carried the title 'Het ontstaan van de Profetische boeken des Ouden Verbonds', and in the first part of his *De godsdienst van Israël* of 1869. These two Dutch works together with the second edition of Ewald's *Die Propheten des Alten Bundes* and a work by Gustav Baur were reviewed by Smith in his long article 'Prophecy in the Critical Schools of the Continent' in 1870.[16]

Smith devoted most of the article to a comparison between Ewald and Kuenen, whom he designated as representatives of believing criticism and rationalist criticism respectively. An early paragraph summed up this comparison:

> Ewald is ready to ascribe to the prophet a spiritual insight into the course of Jahveh's purpose which no man could attain by mere natural reasoning…Kuenen, on the other hand, would have everything explained by the psychology of ordinary life. He ascribes to the prophet [Amos] no really new creative thought.[17]

Now it would be easy for us to conclude that the preference which Smith evinces in this essay for Ewald over Kuenen is simply a function of the fact that Smith and Ewald were believers while Kuenen was

16. See n. 15.
17. Smith, 'Prophecy in the Critical Schools', p. 169.

apparently not.[18] But this would be unjust to Smith; and it brings us to something that was central to his position. Kuenen posed for Smith a very simple problem: if the religion of the prophets was basically a human achievement, why was it apparently unmatched anywhere else in the ancient world? How did it come about that no other religious group had arrived at a conception of God that lifted the deity far above the interests of the nation, making in the process claims about God's universal sovereignty that would embrace all nations?

Smith quoted Kuenen's position from a passage from the *Onderzoek* as follows:

> ...the prophecy of Israel is a product of the religious disposition of the nation as it developed itself under the guidance of its fortunes and the continuous influence of God's Spirit. The prophets are *geniuses* or *heroes* in the ethico-religious field, produced by Israel in the same sense as every nation produces its great men. They differ from other Semitic prophets in degree, not in kind. The difference corresponds to the high superiority of the Israelitish religion, and like the latter must be explained by the providential co-operation of national spirit and national history.[19]

Smith was quick to point out that this sounded more religious than was the case. The reference to 'the continuous influence of God's spirit' was, in practice, only another way of describing national disposition; and where Kuenen spoke of divine inspiration he had in mind those states of ecstasy where a prophet was seized by Jahveh or Baal or Ashera, and out of this excitement and state of half-consciousness expressed 'the testimony of the Godhead in his inner man'.[20]

Kuenen's view of Israelite prophecy was that it had been founded by Samuel, at a time when the survival of Israel was at stake. Samuel combined the belief that Jahveh was Israel's national God with Canaanite ecstatic prophecy, producing bands of prophets with ecstatic enthusiasm for Jahveh. These prophetic bands enabled Israel to survive the threats to its national existence, although by the time of Amos they had lost much of their vigour and influence. With Amos something entirely new appeared in Israelite prophecy: a notion of a God raised above the

---

18. This remark may be unfair to Kuenen. He certainly was a 'modernist' in the context of nineteenth-century Dutch theology.

19. 'Prophecy in the Critical Schools', p. 191, quoting Kuenen's *Historisch-kritisch onderzoek* (Haarlem, 1863), II, p. 27.

20. 'Prophecy in the Critical Schools', p. 193, quoting Kuenen's *De godsdienst van Israël*, p. 187.

national interest, and with moral attributes that separated him from other gods. How did this come about? It resulted, according to Kuenen, from the struggle between the prophetic groups that opposed Ahab and Jezebel, and the latter's attempt to introduce formally into Israel the worship of Baal. In this struggle, the prophets of Jahveh suffered considerably, and thereby gained a deeper sense of the spiritual character of their God. If he was a God for whom they were ready to die, he must be great indeed. The prophets then supported Jehu in his moves to destroy the dynasty of Ahab; but instead of this prophetic revolution producing prosperity, an Israel weakened by civil war fell prey to the Syrian king Hazael. The conclusion was drawn that this setback occurred not because Jahveh was weak, but because he was angry. Thus, his moral attributes transcending national interest were stressed. This view won a place in the heart of earnest worshippers, and especially among the simple nomadic families, to which Amos belonged. From this soil sprung up the great new thoughts that characterized the eighth-century prophets.

Smith found this account of the development of Israelite prophecy totally unsatisfactory and summarized its implications in the following withering paragraph:

> Can we evolve the life-work of the newer prophets from the categories of natural religious feeling, physical enthusiasm, national temperament, historical circumstances? To gain even a show of plausibility for such an attempt, the critic is forced everywhere to look away from the noble spirituality, the lofty comprehensiveness of view, which he cannot deny to the prophets, and seek by a petty pragmatism to bring out into exaggerated prominence the limitations of their natural and religious convictions.[21]

This observation pointed up the implications of different possible historical approaches to prophecy. If the presupposition was that Old Testament prophecy was a purely natural or national phenomenon, then it would be looked at in such a way as to play down its spiritual dimensions and to concentrate on its human features. If Old Testament prophecy was believed to be inspired, its history and achievements would be described somewhat differently. Thus Smith was able to make the following important claim: 'That is not a true historical criticism which does not acknowledge in history a higher element than the merely natural'. And he continued:

---

21. 'Prophecy in the Critical Schools', p. 196.

It is from a criticism that has learned this lesson, that can approach the weighty problems of prophecy from the human side without ignoring the hand of God, that we look for real fruit.[22]

If we reflect on this article we see that Smith was transposing the old apologetic into a new key. The old apologetic saw in the fulfilment of prophecies the proof of their divine origin. Smith saw evidence of divine origin in the spiritual achievements of the prophets in their particular circumstances, achievements which could not be explained in natural terms. In discussing Kuenen's view that Moses borrowed some of his ethical ideas from the Egyptians, Smith asked

why did the Egyptian ethics remain without advance while the same teaching, brought over to a much less cultivated nation, bore fruits so remarkable?[23]

But Smith's article left open three questions that this lecture will need to consider in turn. How, in Smith's view, was prophecy fulfilled, how were prophets inspired, and how did prophecy develop within and influence Israelite history?

The question of the fulfilment of prophecy was dealt with in an Aberdeen lecture of January 1871, which included a critique of J.H. Newman's theory of prophecy, and in the final lecture of the eight lectures which made up *The Prophets of Israel*. It is also alluded to in an 1876 Aberdeen lecture, 'Was Prophecy Supernatural?'.[24]

Smith's starting point is set out in the 1871 lecture, and consists in the fact that the New Testament dispensation is quite different from the Old Testament dispensation. Why did the first followers of Jesus find it so difficult to accept the idea that Jesus was the fulfilment of Scripture? Because he was so different from anything that they had learned to expect. But why was this so? Because the prophets were unable to express their great insights about God's purposes other than by using ideas and images drawn from the religious and political institutions of their own day. Thus, when speaking of the messiah as an ideal David, the prophets speak of him as being a visible ruler over Israel and other

22. 'Prophecy in the Critical Schools', p. 201.
23. 'Prophecy in the Critical Schools', p. 198.
24. For the 1871 lecture see *Lectures and Essays*, pp. 253-84, for the 1876 lecture see *Lectures and Essays*, pp. 349-66. The chapter in *The Prophets of Israel* is pp. 317-73 in the second edition.

nations, of his receiving tribute from the nations, of his going out to battle and smiting his enemies, of his occupying a throne set up on Mt Sion. To quote Smith:

> his features are those of David or Solomon, cleansed from all stain of imperfection, elevated into ideal majesty and illuminated by the unchanging light of God's presence.[25]

Yet this picture cannot be held to be literally fulfilled in Jesus. The two dispensations (of the Old and New Testaments) can only be brought into harmony

> when encumbrances are cleared away, the earthly shell rubbed off, [and] a more comprehensive view [is] gained by the occupation of a higher standpoint.[26]

Indeed, a central question of Old Testament interpretation is

> in what measure is the New Testament dispensation not merely an elevation—an idealisation—of the Old Testament, but something really and qualitatively new, which the Old Testament only shadowed forth without presenting essential identity or even such an identity that the one can flow from the other by mere regular growth?[27]

The answer given by Smith is that the relation between the two Testaments and the dispensations that they represent is one of analogy. The institutions of the Old Testament—kingship, priesthood, sacrifice—played their part in designating and preserving a people that was the object of God's grace. The New Testament situation is quite different, and lacks such things as kingship, priesthood and sacrifice. Yet the same objective is realized by the New Testament dispensation, albeit on an enhanced scale, of designating and preserving a people. When it comes to prophecy the principle of analogy is equally valid, in that the prophets express their intuitions and hopes for the fuller realization of God's sovereignty, in terms necessarily drawn from the world of the Old Testament; but this does not mean that the fulfilment of their prophecies could be literally in terms of the Old Testament institutions. We know, in fact, that the fulfilment was not in terms of Old Testament institutions. Fulfilments had to take a form determined by the historical circumstances of their fulfilment, and thus the essential ideas that were contained in

25. *Lectures and Essays*, p. 254.
26. *Lectures and Essays*, p. 255.
27. *Lectures and Essays*, p. 259.

prophecies assumed new shapes when the time came for their fulfilment.

Smith's approach to fulfilment by way of analogy enabled him to do three things. First, he was able to explain the apparent non-fulfilment of certain prophecies. In the last of his 1881 lectures he discussed the passage in Isa. 19.24-25, which he accepted as the words of Isaiah. The fact that the passage is generally regarded today as secondary does not affect Smith's point. The passage reads:

> In that day shall Israel be the third with Egypt and with Assyria, even a blessing in the midst of the earth, Whom the Lord of Hosts shall bless, saying, Blessed be Egypt my people, and Assyria the work of my hands, and Israel mine inheritance.

Smith's view of this passage was that the prophet looked forward to a decisive event as described in Isa. 19.20, 'he shall send them a saviour, and a great one, and he shall deliver them', which would lead to the conversion of the whole earth to the God of Israel, the whole earth being indicated by the nations Egypt, Assyria and Israel. Now this prophecy was not fulfilled in Isaiah's time; nor was it capable of being fulfilled now.[28] This led to Smith's second main point, which was against looking for the fulfilment today or in the future of unfulfilled Old Testament prophecies. If Isaiah's prophecy were to be fulfilled today, it would restrict God's sovereignty to a tiny part of the world as we know it today—Egypt, Syria-Palestine and Mesopotamia—although this represented the inhabited earth in Isaiah's thought. In any case, Egypt and Assyria as Isaiah knew them no longer existed. As Smith put it trenchantly:

> The forms in which Isaiah enshrined his spiritual hopes are broken, and cannot be restored; they belong to an epoch of history that can never return.[29]

Given this, it is not surprising that Smith reserved some of his most withering rhetoric for those who wished to see modern events as fulfilments of prophecy. He described them as

---

28. Smith, *Prophets of Israel*, p. 337: 'Not only have Isaiah's predictions received no literal fulfilment, but it is impossible that the evolution of the divine purpose can ever again be narrowed within the limits of the petty world of which Judah was the centre and Egypt and Assyria the extremes'.

29. *Prophets of Israel*, p. 337.

Fanciful theorists who use the Old Testament as a book of curious
mysteries, and profane its grandeur by adapting it to their idle visions at
the sacrifice of every law of sound hermeneutics and sober historical
judgment.[30]

He was also scathing about those who looked for a restoration of Jews
to Palestine as part of a future consummation of God's kingdom; and in
an earlier lecture he taunted such people with the vision of the restored
temple and its animal sacrificial system found in Ezekiel 40–48.[31] If this
was yet to be fulfilled, what would St Paul make of it?

Smith was especially concerned to refute a mid-way position, which
was that it might be possible to look for a present or future fulfilment
for prophecies, some of whose details might be more capable of being
reconciled with the march of history. No, averred Smith. The full implications of the failure of the literalist view of prophecy had to be drawn.

This brings us to Smith's third point under this heading, namely, his
insistence that accepting the variety of dispensations in God's dealing
with humanity made it possible to see absolutely clearly God's unity of
purpose. Once the literalist fallacy had been disposed of, once the
insights of the prophets were seen to be necessarily expressed in the
forms of language and ideas of their times, forms of language and ideas
that would not be appropriate to later situations, it was possible to see
the essence of what they were saying, and to see how it referred beyond
itself in articulating God's purpose.

Smith makes it clear that this essence of prophecy is not the spiritual
sense of Scripture as understood by medieval exegesis and modern
Protestantism.[32] According to that view, everything in Scripture has a
meaning, and if that meaning is obscure or not fulfilled, this is a deliberate piece of mystification by the Holy Spirit, to be de-mystified in the
future. Smith's position is that prophetic utterances were subject to real
limitations, the limitations of time, circumstance and understanding. Yet
it is precisely when the words of the prophets are taken for what they
are, namely, ordinary human speech directed to the circumstances of the
prophets' times, that their true spiritual significance can be appreciated.
In the case of Isaiah, Smith sums up this spiritual significance as follows:

30. *Prophets of Israel*, p. 337.
31. *Lectures and Essays*, p. 256.
32. *Prophets of Israel*, pp. 339ff.

The kingship of Jehovah, the holy majesty of the one true God, the eternal validity of His law of righteousness, the certainty that His cause on earth is imperishable and must triumph over all the wrath of man, that His word of grace cannot be without avail, and that the community of His grace is the one thing on earth that cannot be brought to nought,—these are the spiritual certainties the possession of which constituted Isaiah a true prophet.[33]

Before leaving this section on the fulfilment of prophecy, it is worth noting how Smith dealt with Newman's view that prophecy had been fulfilled in the sense that, whereas Israel was a visible manifestation of God's kingdom on earth under the old dispensation, so the Catholic church was the kingdom's visible manifestation on earth under the new dispensation.[34] Smith, not surprisingly, rejected the identification of the church with the kingdom of God; but his main objection was that Newman's approach was a sophisticated, and thus dangerously seductive, version of the literalist view of fulfilment. Smith devoted part of the last Burnett Lecture to repeating his objections to Newman.[35]

I come now to Smith's view of prophetic inspiration, a view closely connected with Smith's understanding of the inspiration of the Bible. In the second lecture I pointed out that Smith held that the Bible was the record of a revelation, not the revelation itself; the writing of inspired men rather than an inspired writing. We can make the same observation about his approach to prophecy. The prophetic books are the record of the words and writings of inspired men, rather than inspired writings. If this seems to be a hair-splitting distinction, it has, in fact, important consequences.

If the prophetic books are inspired writings, how are they inspired? Are the writers merely passive recorders of God's words? Does the Holy Spirit guide their thoughts or even their pens as they write? If, as is obvious, the writers have their individual styles and modes of expression, how does this individuality combine with divine inspiration? This kind of approach had, so far as Smith was concerned, been once and for all disposed of in Richard Rothe's *Zur Dogmatik*.[36]

Smith preferred to see inspiration in terms of the personal relationship that granted to the prophets insights about the nature and purpose of God that were not mere information *about* God, but actual knowledge

33. *Prophets of Israel*, pp. 340-41.
34. See *Lectures and Essays*, pp. 266ff.
35. Cambridge University Library ADD 7476 H13.
36. See above, pp. 89-92.

of God. How Smith expressed this we shall see shortly. First, we must note that Smith firmly rejected two popular views of how the prophets related to God. The first was that the relationship was one of ecstasy, a view espoused by Kuenen in the light of his opinion that Israelite prophecy borrowed features from Canaanite prophecy.[37] Smith rejected this because the Old Testament seemed to indicate that if the prophets influenced their contemporaries, it was through their words and deeds that bore the 'stamp of a vigorous, healthy, waking life'. Smith added:

> The theory of ecstasy is an attempt to divide the prophet from the prophetic word, while in truth the peculiar power of men like Amos and Isaiah lay just in the thoroughness with which the word of Jahveh filled and elevated the natural personality of the speaker.[38]

The view that the prophetic revelations were associated with visions had been revived by Hengstenberg and, according to Smith, had 'left no inconsiderable mark on the conservative theology of Germany'.[39] However, in dealing with Isaiah's inaugural vision, Smith pointed out that visions were of very rare occurrence in the experience of the greatest prophets.[40] He also argued, on psychological grounds, that visions and dreams result from the free wandering of the imagination over what is stored in the memory, so that a dream or vision could only supply something new by freshly combining what already lay in the memory. This was different from prophecy, where new insights came to a prophet from his relationship with God.

The clearest account of this process of divine illumination that I have found in Smith's writings is as follows:

> We must seek the true mark of the prophet…in the personal sympathy between himself and Jahveh, by virtue of which the God-sent thought approves itself to him inwardly, and not by mere external authority…The prophet presents himself to the critical inquirer, less in the light of one who is the passive subject of supernatural influence, than as a man whose life and thoughts are determined by personal fellowship with Jahveh and by intelligent insight into his purpose.[41]

---

37. *Lectures and Essays*, p. 185.
38. *Lectures and Essays*, p. 185.
39. *Lectures and Essays*, p. 185.
40. *Prophets of Israel*, p. 221.
41. *Lectures and Essays*, p. 186.

The insight that came from fellowship with God gave the prophet a standpoint that differed from that of his contemporaries when it came to interpreting the events of the day. In an interesting passage on Isaiah Smith rejects the view that, if we today had lived in the times when God actually proved himself to be a living God, we would have had no difficulty in believing. Smith denies that

> it would have been easy to believe, or rather impossible not to do so, because the supernatural in those days was as palpable to the senses as natural phenomena are now.[42]

This was not true simply because, as the story of Isaiah's confrontation with Ahaz at the time of the Syro-Ephraimite threat shows, the events that gave Isaiah an assurance that God was present among his people were precisely the same events that filled Ahaz with despair and made him turn for help to Assyria.

This leads us to the final section of the lecture, Smith's account of the history of prophecy in Israel, or at any rate its history in regard to the eighth-century prophets.

By the time that he published *The Prophets of Israel* Smith had accepted the view that the levitical legislation attributed in Exodus, Leviticus and Numbers to Moses was not written until the post-exilic period. Nonetheless Smith retained for Moses a contribution to Israel's religion that was important for prophecy.[43] It was Moses who was crucially involved in, and who decisively interpreted, the deliverance of the Israelites from Egypt. The teaching about God that he imparted to the Israelites was not teaching about abstract divine attributes; it was an assurance of God's personal interest in Israel. But this interest had practical implications. The Israelites were to be united as a nation and united in their loyalty to God. God had given them liberty; but he required in return law, justice and the moral order of society.

This Mosaic faith had to adapt itself to the conditions of life in Canaan, and Smith sketches the way in which popular Israelite religion came to resemble that of the Canaanites. He deals with the period of the Judges and of Samuel, Saul and David in less than four pages, and commenting further that little is known of the history of Israel's religion between Solomon and Ahab, fastens on to Elijah as the true successor of Moses. Elijah, as a native of Trans-jordanian Gilead, had affinity with the nomad

42. *Prophets of Israel*, p. 270.
43. *Prophets of Israel*, pp. 32ff.

life of the time of Moses. He applied the Mosaic religion to the new circumstances of Jezebel's attempt to make Israel officially adopt the religion of Baal. In particular, in condemning Ahab for unjustly seizing Naboth's vineyard, Elijah upheld the essential heart of the religion of Jehovah:

> The sovereignty of Jehovah was not an empty thought; it was the refuge of the oppressed, the support of the weak against the mighty…if Jehovah claimed Israel as His dominion, in which no other god could find a place, He did so because His rule was the rule of absolute righteousness.[44]

This, according to Smith, was not only a lesson unknown to Ahab; it was unheeded by Jehu, who was anointed by Elisha to destroy Ahab's dynasty. Smith, wrongly in my view, dissociates Elijah from the prophetic groups presided over by Elisha, and sees these groups and Jehu's dynasty as 'sinking to depths of hypocrisy and formalism'. However, Smith rightly sketches the injustices and oppression of the poor that characterized the later rulers of Jehu's dynasty in the eighth century and which form the background to the work of Hosea and Amos.

Smith's picture of Amos is in a sense contradictory, a point which he implicitly acknowledges but does not resolve satisfactorily. On the one hand we have a man from a village that is not one of the centres of life of his country, a man 'nurtured in austere simplicity', who in the vast solitudes where he pastured his flock heard the voice of God: 'Go prophesy to my people Israel' (Amos 7.15). On the other hand we have a man whose language evinces one of the best examples of pure Hebrew style and whose outlook displays a breadth of human interest based on a range of historical observation very remarkable in the age and condition of the author.[45] How could Amos be so isolated and independent and at the same time so accomplished and informed? Smith appealed to Arabia and to an analogy between Hebrew and Arabian society, where 'knowledge and oratory were not affairs of professional education, or dependent for their cultivation on wealth and social status'.[46] Smith summed up Amos's message as an announcement of swift impending judgment on a nation and rulers who had forgotten their responsibilities as God's people. That God should be about to do this to Israel would

---

44. *Prophets of Israel*, p. 87.
45. *Prophets of Israel*, p. 127.
46. *Prophets of Israel*, p. 126.

have been shocking to a people still accustomed to thinking of their God as existing to protect them against other nations. But Amos had a deep insight into the will of God for justice among all nations; and if God was going to punish Damascus, Ammon and Moab for committing atrocities against their neighbours, so he was going to punish Israel for committing injustice against its own people. He was also going to teach his people who he was by means of prophetically interpreted events of their history.

Smith's treatment of Hosea will sound familiar to anyone who has studied Hosea at school; but this will be partly a result of Smith's influence directly or indirectly upon biblical studies. It is today a commonplace to understand Hosea's teaching about God in the light of his marriage to Gomer, a marriage in which his wife deserted him, became a prostitute and then a slave, before being bought back by the prophet. In Smith's day this approach was known (it had been endorsed by Ewald, albeit on the theory that part of the story had been lost from chs. 1–3)[47] but it was by no means widely accepted, and in some circles it was vigorously opposed on the grounds that God would not commission a prophet to do something immoral, such as marrying a prostitute.[48] Smith dealt with this latter point very simply. Hosea did not know that Gomer was going to desert him and become a prostitute, it was out of the agony of this discovery that he learned something of God's own feeling towards Israel.[49]

Smith made noteworthy points about Hosea. First, by speaking about God's covenant with Israel in terms of love, Hosea took an idea that was to be found in the religions of Israel's neighbours and gave it a new dimension.[50] For Israel's neighbours, love was a physical thing and expressed a natural relationship between a god and its people. Hosea stressed the moral aspect of love and thereby articulated a relationship between Jehovah and Israel that transcended the natural and the national. Secondly, Smith pointed out how Hosea condemned the bloodshed of

47. Ewald, *Propheten des Alten Bundes*, I, pp. 182-84.

48. See, for example, Samuel Davidson in T.H. Horne's *An Introduction to the Critical Study and Knowledge of the Holy Scriptures* (London, 10th edn, 1859), II, p. 943. Davidson follows Hengstenberg in rejecting the interpretation later advanced by Smith. A good overview of British scholarly opinion in the mid-nineteenth century on this matter is in the article 'Hosea' in William Smith's *Dictionary of the Bible* (London, 1863), I, p. 831.

49. *Prophets of Israel*, pp. 181-82.

50. *Prophets of Israel*, p. 175.

the revolution that brought Jehu to power, supported by Elisha and his prophets.[51] This enabled Smith to emphasize that there was no mechanical uniformity in the teaching of the prophets; that what one might approve of, another might condemn. There are echoes here of Rothe's view that no one person or writing can give a complete account of God's nature or will.

The remainder of the *Prophets of Israel* deals with Isaiah and Jeremiah, the former in by far the greater detail. Again, Smith deliberately contrasts them in pursuit of his (Rothian) view that prophets are inspired men whose message is particular to the situation of each. Thus both Isaiah and Jeremiah saw the existence of the nation threatened by neighbouring powers, but took opposite views about the outcome.[52] Isaiah was convinced that the survival of Judah was necessary if God was to accomplish his purpose; Jeremiah believed that Judah needed to go into exile in order to further God's plan. Both prophets were correct within the context of their situations.

For Smith, the guiding power of Isaiah's work was his vision of the holiness of God which he saw in his call to be a prophet.[53] This gave him a sense of the universal power of God and his concern for justice, a sense of God which put the national interests of Judah into a new light. In the incident in which Hezekiah encouraged Isaiah to stand firm against the Assyrians, Isaiah was not acting as a naive believer in God's power nor as a traitor to Judah's national survival. Isaiah was concerned with something more than mere national survival. He was concerned with the religious and moral condition of the people, concerned that the holiness of God should be reflected in how the nation ordered its life in conformity to God's will. To have the nation survive so that it continued to practice injustice and idolatry was no part of Isaiah's agenda.[54] Although, at the end of the day, Isaiah believed that the survival of Judah was God's will, his convictions about what mattered most were passed on to Jeremiah, who drew the conclusion in his day that only the destruction of Judah could provide the opportunity for the creation of a people of God respecting justice and religion.

Of all Smith's work on the Old Testament, that on prophecy seems the most dated today, for one simple and surprising reason. The man

---

51. *Prophets of Israel*, p. 184.
52. *Prophets of Israel*, p. 259.
53. *Prophets of Israel*, p. 225.
54. *Prophets of Israel*, p. 325.

who is honoured among anthropologists and sociologists for having put the study of religion on a new footing was apparently completely idealistic when it came to studying the prophets. Amos and Hosea are inspired individuals with no connection with prophetic guilds. Indeed, the isolation of Amos from society (in spite of his oriental educatedness) is his greatest qualification for being a prophet. The same is true of Elijah, whose isolation from the culture of his day and his closeness to the nomadic Mosaic traditions are emphasized by Smith.

However, to criticize Smith's approach to prophecy as 'idealistic' is to fail to see his greatness in the context of his day. At a time when, only fifty years earlier, conferences had been held to determine which Old Testament prophecies remained to be fulfilled in the present and the future, Smith boldly asserted that those attempts fundamentally misunderstood the relation between the old and new dispensations, and demeaned rather than respected the prophets. There were no Old Testament prophecies still awaiting fulfilment. Yet this seemingly negative stance was part of a series of arguments designed to affirm as strongly as possible that the prophets were inspired by God and played a vital part in interpreting to the Israelites how God was present in the events of their history. In turn, this claim became a powerful apologetic for Christianity, as Smith challenged his opponents to consider the vast difference between the moral and religious teaching of Israel's prophets and the religions of Israel's far more culturally developed neighbours. It was a bold and powerful theological synthesis the like of which had not been seen in British theology previously, and which has hardly been matched since.

Chapter 8

SMITH THE PREACHER

'I never preach now.' Whether it was with sadness, relief or resignation that Robertson Smith confided this information to a friend in December 1885 we shall presumably never know.[1] The fact is, however, that for twelve years of his life Smith was an active preacher, and his sermons are not only interesting in themselves but provide important clues to the development of his thought.

Smith's biographers devote a page and a half to Smith's preaching, the substance of which can be summarized as follows. Because his youth and lack of practical experience of ministry had been cited as an argument against his appointment to his chair in 1870, Smith began to accept preaching engagements in 1870 immediately after his appointment to the post (which was on 25 May) and before the formal beginning of his duties on 3 November. He wanted to show that he would be fully committed to this aspect of the active service of his church. Smith's preaching is described by the biographers as conventional, and it is noted that people who went to hear him preach during the period of controversy from 1876 to 1880 were often disappointed with the old-fashioned evangelicalism that they heard. The following quotation from a hearer of three sermons of Smith, part of which I shall reproduce, is said to be 'a just appreciation of Smith's characteristics as a preacher'.

> I have heard Smith preach three times now. Bonar was with me once, and did not quite like it; the references to Christ seemed too expressly orthodox, he thought, to be the genuine expression of his belief. But of course B[onar] knows nothing of theology, and presumes that Smith must diverge from the orthodox throughout, because he is so enlightened a critic of the

---

1.   Smith to a friend, usually taken to be the Rev. B. Bell, Cambridge University Library ADD 7476 M10, p. 10. The implications of this for understanding Smith are discussed in Chapter 9, p. 149 below.

Book. I suppose he is quite orthodox on the Person and Work of Christ. I have thought his preaching interesting and full of wise, and often delicately suggestive, practical teaching, and I have been struck with what seemed a tender reverence of tone in his whole service, spite of [*sic*] the natural irreverence of his voice.[2]

As far as I am aware, only one of Smith's sermons was published, that preached in St George's Free Church in Edinburgh in May 1877.[3] The Smith archive in Cambridge contains 62 numbered items,[4] of which one is a misplaced sheet from another sermon, one is notes for a lecture on David Hume and quite a few are fragments, or notes from which it is impossible to reconstruct in any detail what Smith might have said.[5] When these are subtracted, there are about 26 sermons that exist either completely or in sufficent detail to make them comprehensible. In eight cases, the dates and places of preaching are listed, and this yields some interesting data.

Smith's favourite sermon, that is, the one he delivered on more occasions than any other, was on Gal. 1.10: 'For do I now persuade men, or God? or do I seek to please men? for if I yet pleased men, I should not be the servant of Christ'. This was preached 23 times between 1872 and 1881, and must have taken on a quite different significance after 1876 when Smith was on trial. The next most frequently preached sermon, 19 times, was on Eph. 4.15: 'But speaking the truth in love, may grow up into him in all things, which is the head, even Christ', and again spans most of Smith's preaching ministry, from 1871 to 1880. If we add up

2.   Black and Chrystal, *Life of William Robertson Smith*, p. 125. The identity of Bonar is not certain. It *may* have been Horatius Bonar, best known now for his hymns.

3.   W.R. Smith, *Sermon Preached in St George's Free Church, Edinburgh on the Afternoon of Sabbath, 27th May 1877* (Edinburgh, 1877). In fact this sermon, preached during a meeting of the General Assembly of the Free Church, is hardly representative of Smith's sermons. An exposition of the story of Jesus and Zacchaeus in Lk. 19.1-10, it certainly does deserve Black and Chrystal's verdict of exhibiting old-fashioned evangelicalism, and it is tempting to see this as an attempt on Smith's part to convince his critics of his orthodoxy.

4.   In what follows, the references are to the Cambridge University Library ADD 7476 Section K.

5.   Thus the single sheet catalogued as K19 is in fact p. 3 of K22, and the lecture notes on Hume are K49. K56 appears to be missing. There are also several versions or drafts of the same sermon, for example K30 and 31 on 1 Cor. 3.10-15 and K42-44 on Heb. 12.14.

the occasions listed by Smith they come to exactly one hundred. Given the roughly twelve years of his preaching activity, from 1870 to 1881, this works out at an average of one sermon every six weeks. But we must remember that Smith spent periods abroad, such as in Göttingen in 1872 (where he delivered several addresses to his entourage and others) and in Egypt and the Hejaz for six months from November 1879 to May 1880. If we subtract these periods, and add in the sermons that are not dated with place and time, we can conclude that Smith preached on average once a month, even if he did reuse sermons. We can also surmise that Smith was under too much pressure of work to feel able to prepare new sermons; but it also follows that in 1880 he was happy with the theological content of sermons that he had prepared eight years previously. A final statistic may be of interest. A word count of the sermons that exist as complete booklets shows them to average about 5000 words. Depending on how rapidly Smith read them, we can guess that he preached for around 40 minutes.

In reviewing Smith's extant sermons the obvious place to begin is with the most frequently preached sermon, that on Gal. 1.10.[6] According to Smith's notes, it was sketched while he was in Göttingen in July 1872 and was written in Keig in April 1873. It is also possibly the last sermon that he preached, since its last recorded date is 6 March 1881, just over two months before his dismissal.

The sermon is pastoral and practical. It recognizes that Christians have to live out their lives in a world whose standards and values may not be those of Christ. Smith is aware of two temptations that may result: that Christians may curry favour with their less-than-Christian neighbours or that they may withdraw from contact with their neighbours in an attempt to keep themselves pure. Towards the end of the sermon Smith addresses the latter with a typical piece of rhetoric:

> It seems indeed almost absurd that those who profess themselves followers of him who poured out his life so freely for sinners, who thought that even his divine existence found its worthiest energy in entering into fellowship with mankind...it seems...absurd that the followers of such a Lord should need to be warned against shutting themselves up within themselves and fancying that it is by isolating their spiritual life that they best ensure its purity and health.

6.   K33.

Christianity, then, was faced with a paradox that has often been summed up in the words (not used by Smith here) about being in the world but not of the world.

How does Smith advise his hearers? He begins by noting a paradox in Paul, whose words about not being pleasers of men are the text for the sermon. Paul had also spoken about becoming 'all things to all men'. How can that be reconciled with not being pleasers of men? The answer is in the second part of the text that opposes being a pleaser of man to being a servant of Christ; and this enables Smith to enunciate the heart of the matter:

> Freedom from the service of man only through the service of Christ—or at least the service of Christ the only true and sure way of deliverance from the service and fear of man.[7]

Smith now gives practical advice under three main points—incidentally, a practice rare rather than common in his sermons. Under the first heading, he acknowledges that, as human beings, people have many social relationships that are proper in that they treat others as ends and not means. But, and at this point we meet an idea that recurs in Smith's interpretation of the religion of Israel,[8] natural relationships become corrupted if they are not purified by true religion. Apart from the service of Christ the tendency to treat others as means rather than as ends becomes strong. Smith describes the outcome:

> the real tyranny of the service of manpleasing which runs through natural society is just that we are constantly constrained to do this, that or the other thing, not because the action has any value towards God or man—but merely because usage and custom demand it of us...This is a real slavery because it disturbs the free working of an independent plan of life.

Smith points out, tellingly, how slaves in the ancient world could have no plans of their own.

He then goes on to address how a number of things such as hospitality and food and drink, which in themselves are not evil, can cross the line from moderation and become occasions for 'manpleasing', if Christians feel compelled to conform to social custom out of fear of how they will

---

7.   The quotation indicates that Smith did not read this as it now stands; for it is hardly grammatical. The sermon notes are a mixture of sections that were read verbatim and of notes that Smith must have elaborated extempore. In a few cases, the sermons contain a full text that could be read in its entirety.

8.   See p. 174.

be regarded if they do not conform. He extends his illustrations from food and drink through dress, recreations and amusements to the Lord's Day. On the latter he says: 'It is often not easy to draw the line between a day of sacred rest and a day of self-seeking rest'.

In the second and third main sections, Smith acknowledges that most people have little control over what they do in their daily work, and that they have power only over their life outside of work. However, the Christian perspective is to see all of life as a calling, as an invitation to occupy a unique place in the work of the kingdom of God. As Smith says, 'to enjoy a life work which we can pursue with such confidence and calmness implies peace and harmony with God'. Thus, towards the end of the sermon, Smith can make the following appeal to his hearers:

> Do you try to live your whole life as a life prescribed to you by Him? Is it always your object to know what your Maker would have you to do, to bring all things to the test of the service of his Kingdom?

Although this was Smith's most frequently preached sermon, it was not one of his best in my opinion. It deserves several observations. The first is its stress upon the kingdom of God as the sphere in which the service of Christ is to be worked out in the world. We remember that the sermon was sketched in Göttingen, where Smith had heard and had become well known to Albrecht Ritschl, and that Ritschl had linked the kingdom of God with the doctrine of Justification.[9] It is not going too far to see the influence of Ritschl here, and in other sermons that speak of the kingdom of God, and to this extent the comment of Smith's biographers, that his sermons could have 'been delivered by any ortho-dox country minister to any Scottish congregation', is probably incorrect.[10] Secondly, during the years of Smith's trials, the sermon must have taken on new meaning for him and his hearers. He preached it on nine occasions between April 1877 and March 1881, and it surely must have reinforced his resolve to stick to the truth as he saw it, and not to acquiesce in attempts to make him conform to what was expected. According to Ritschl, and, indeed, to Protestant orthodoxy, the church and the kingdom of God were not the same thing, and Smith, loyal though he was to his church, had to pledge his fullest loyalty to the kingdom and its king.

There is a sermon directly on the kingdom of God, first preached on

9.　See p. 77
10.　Black and Chrystal, *Life of William Robertson Smith*, p. 124.

19 June 1870 and preached six times in all, the text being from Mt. 6.33, 'Seek ye first the Kingdom of God and his righteousness'.[11] The sermon opens with a powerful indictment of all human activity which, however noble in itself, is inadequte if it is not done for God's glory:

> man has sought for himself a selfish end which is not God's end. He is doing work which however noble and even spiritual it may seem is not God's work...Even to preserve through a few short years that body which is no longer an instrument for God's service unbroken by the relentless sweep of the machinery of a hostile universe is a task that calls from day to day for all the care and thought that man can muster, a task so absorbing that it may fairly be called the one work of fallen man.

Smith attacks the idea that there is a natural kingdom of God based upon a natural Fatherhood of God and a natural providence. Such ideas are foreign to the Bible, which knows only of relationships brought about by God. Israel's special status

> lay on the knowledge that man can never himself find God as a loving God: that Abraham's seed had no more right than the Gentiles to claim God as their Father, but that God of his free grace had drawn nigh to the people of Israel redeeming them out of Egypt...entering into a Covenant with them.

The special relationship between God and Israel was defined in terms of the ritual law which governed the smallest steps of the daily walk. The prophets, however, saw that these were merely outward marks of the special relationship and not its essence. The same problem is found when Christians try to define themselves by outward observances such as religious exercises and abstinences.

Smith thus addresses himself to a matter which remains as problematic today as when he first preached. If Christianity implies a unique relationship between a community and God, how is that uniqueness to be expressed without assuming distinctive characteristics that cut it off from the rest of society or that become merely external marks without a corresponding inner spirit? Smith does not give a direct answer but rather expresses his faith that God is at work to establish his kingdom among humanity. His definition of the kingdom is a noble one:

> The Kingdom must be as wide as humanity itself. It is not designed for reasons that we cannot fathom, to embrace every unit of the human race; but it is designed to contain within itself the whole compass of man's life,

11. K16.

to show its power of annihilating all that is sinful in every corner of human society, of regenerating and turning towards God's glory every fruit of man's thought and man's labour, however mean and insignificant it may seem.

This kingdom thus defined was something that Smith could urge his hearers to enter, in the name of Christ. Jesus says that the gate of the kingdom is wide enough for us 'but too strait to admit a burden along with you'. Leave all and follow me. 'Every lawful vocation to which God in his providence calls men has some bearing on the development of his Kingdom.'

While we are dealing with sermons on the kingdom of God, of which there are several more, it is worth noting two in which the influence of Ritschl can be discerned. The first is an undated set of notes of four sides of paper, on Mt. 5.3: 'Blessed are the poor in spirit'.[12] Part of the notes is a technical discussion of the fact that one single Hebrew word *'ani* can express the two Greek words *ptochoi* (poor) and *praeis* (meek). This enables Smith to see the meek or righteous poor in the Old Testament as the ones to whom the kingdom is promised, and who are thus both mentioned in Matthew 5. But there is another noble passage written out in full among the notes, and it has strong Ritschlian overtones:

> Jesus preaches the coming of the *Kingdom* but preaches it as a *moral* Kingdom to be entered by repentance...his preaching cannot consist of mere admonition to *individuals*. He speaks to the citizens of the Kingdom— as a class...The poor, meek respectively shall be raised to sovereignty in the earth when on earth the Spiritual Kingdom is set up. The approach of the Kingdom is the setting up on earth of a real though not a causal sovereignty whereby the Dominion belongs no more to the great and mighty tyrants of the world but to the *ptochoi praeis*.

The other sermon to be noted here, again an early one written in Autumn 1870 and given on ten occasions between then and August 1874, is on Mt. 20.28: 'The Son of Man came not be be ministered unto, but to minister and to give his life a ransom for many'.[13] This sermon approaches the doctrine of Christ's death via that of the kingdom of God based on a death voluntarily undergone. Since Christ laid down his life to establish the kingdom we are connected with Christ's death when we enter the kingdom by repentance. There is a central passage in this sermon in note form, and by way of one of the

12. K14.
13. K18.

revisions and supplementations in reddish ink which are occasionally to be found in the manuscripts. The passage reads:

> A lot of us wanting Christ without proper surrender, etc. e.g. we still propose to follow him in a way of our own choosing. We are willing to give up our own sinful desires and loves if only God will help us in our innocent desires. The salvation for which we long is not a new life made strong to follow new ends, but our old life sweetened purified and strengthened by the assurance that God will make our path smooth towards the attainment of our harmless personal ends and the satisfaction of our natural personal interests.[14]

I now turn to something different, to sermons on three Psalms, one of which is dated to Smith's visit to Göttingen in the summer of 1872, and the others of which are probably early, given the critical positions that they take. The dated sermon—Göttingen, 21 July 1872—is on Psalm 32 and seems either to exist in three versions or to consist of several drafts.[15] It begins with a surprise. The Psalm was composed by David. Smith bases this claim not on the title 'A Psalm of David' but on the content. It is the old poem of a famous poet, and shows us the inner side of David's experience. It also shows us that the experience of joy and peace with God is no less real in the Old Testament than in the New Testament, even if it is less generally clear in the Old Testament. A point noted in particular is that David has this experience *without* the need for the Old Testament priestly mechanisms of sacrifice and atonement.

In applying the Psalm to contemporary beliefs, Smith distinguishes its teaching from two particular Christian emphases. The first is the experience of conversion. The Psalm does not deal with this. David is not now for the first time learning to trust in God. He had fallen from grace and now discovers how, through confessing his sins, he can regain a joyful sense of forgiveness and peace. The second contrast made by Smith is with the pietistic *Busskampf*, a subject discussed by Albrecht Ritschl in the third volume of his work on Justification.[16] *Busskampf* was a great

14. Although it is wrong to press an argument from silence too far, one interesting fact about Smith's sermons is that there is not one about the expiatory benefits of Christ's death on the cross. Sermon K18 is the only sermon that is on a text that could have been treated in this way. Instead, Smith chose to link Christ's death to the establishment of the kingdom of God.

15. K4.

16. A. Ritschl, *Die christliche Lehre von der Rechtfertigung und Versöhnung* (Bonn, 1874), III, p. 139. The volume postdates Smith's Göttingen visit but presumably Smith had heard Ritschl speak on this matter.

crisis of alienation from God which preceded the experience of new birth; but it was also a daily or regular exercise of self-loathing designed to be followed by a feeling of relief, which in turn was an assurance of salvation. As such, it easily degenerated into a legalistic 'work'. Smith saw none of this in the Psalm. The conviction of forgiveness does not rest upon the feeling of relief that follows the pietistic *Busskampf* but on God's own promise, on God's own revelation.

Another of the sermons is on Psalm 90, and although undated is presumably early, in that Smith accepts the claim of the title that it was written by Moses.[17] Even if it was not, it reflects his thoughts towards the end of the forty years of wandering in the wilderness. The Psalm is thus read in the context of Deut. 1.34-39, where Moses is informed that he will not enter the promised land but that a new generation led by Joshua will enter it. Smith considers how this news would affect Moses, the man of fiery energy, the man who would be robbed of his ambition to enter the Promised Land because of the sins of the people, a people for whom God had richly provided.

However, the source of Moses' zeal is his faith, and thus he is able to trust that God will fulfil his purposes through others. His faith is not quenched, but purified and softened by this experience. Smith uses the Psalm to draw lessons about the nature of prayer in general. Prayer is a bringing of our sinful weakness to God so that he can do all for us, in the knowledge that he does not forsake his own. However, it begins with an expression of trust and hope—'Lord, thou hast been our dwelling place in all generations'—before it turns to the trials and pathos of Moses' position. There is a great contrast between the unchangeable God and the weak and fleeting man, who appears for but a moment to form one slight link in the chain of God's purpose.

The other sermon on the Psalms deals with Psalm 73.[18] Because it is mostly in note form on three and a half sides it may well be a later sermon, and it deals with a favourite theme of Smith—the Christian doctine of providence. He denies that there is a real providence outside of God's covenant relationship with his people; and since the covenant is God's gracious gift yet designed to carry forward *his* purposes, the link between providence and covenant makes it impossible for us to see providence as simply something for our convenience. As Smith says:

17.   K7 (and also K8).
18.   K6.

> God's providence is not merely a supplement to that which we do and aim
> at ourselves...God on [the] one hand calls us [to] do nothing for ourselves
> and all for him and he on the other hand will do all for us.

Smith's linking of providence and covenant enables him to express his
conviction that all the processes of world history will reach their culmination according to the purposes revealed in Christ: 'Christ is moulding
all the earth to himself—with all its knowledge, its industry, its affections;
all but its sin and the fount of its sin'.

I propose next to discuss two sermons where we can see Smith the
scholar overshadowing Smith the preacher. The first, undated, is on Mk
11.1-10, the triumphal entry of Jesus into Jerusalem.[19] Presumably it
was written for a Palm Sunday; but it presented Smith with a problem
that had long intrigued him, namely, the fulfilment of prophecy.[20] Mark,
of course, says nothing about a link between the riding on an ass and the
prophecy of Zech. 9.9; but Matthew and John do; and there is also an
interesting difference between John and the other Gospels. In the other
Gospels the crowd take up their palm branches and cry 'Hosanna!'
when they see Jesus riding on the ass. In John, the order is reversed. The
crowd come to meet Jesus, carrying their palm branches and shouting
'Hosanna!', whereupon Jesus finds and mounts an ass, in accordance
with what is written in Zech. 9.9.

Smith was convinced that the account in John was both the more
accurate account and the one that made it possible to see how the
fulfilment of the prophecy was to be understood. Unusually for his
sermons, we suddenly hear the language of the lecture hall or the
academic essay rather than of the pulpit:

> Jesus seems to have sent for the ass after he observed the reception which
> the multitude was preparing for him. The last inference from John's
> language is not perhaps necessary: but is in itself plausible and may I
> think be raised to certainty when we observe that from the two hints of
> John the whole episode may be understood with a clearness that leaves
> nothing to be desired.

How, then, was the prophecy fulfilled? Not by accident. Jesus did not
procure the ass because he was tired, thereby fulfilling Zech. 9.9 in spite
of himself. Nor did he set out deliberately to achieve a fulfilment. Rather,
the initiative of the crowds in welcoming him as a king demanded a

19. K22.
20. See Chapter 7, pp. 119-23.

course of action that would *subvert* these expectations and show what was the true nature of his kingdom and kingship. This was why he mounted the ass, thereby drawing on the symbolism of that animal and of its role in Zech. 9.9.

This sermon, with its scholarly ingenuity, is one of the least successful of Smith's sermons if we judge a sermon by its appeal to the heart and imagination and not just to the intellect. The same cannot be said of the sermon on 1 Kings 12–13, the story of Jeroboam's rebellion and of the prophet who was killed because he was persuaded by another prophet to disobey God.[21] This sermon is one of the later dated sermons; it was first delivered in Keig in the autumn of 1877 and then was given a further nine times. The last occasion was in Kelvinside, Glasgow, on 26 December 1880; and if we feel that it was not obviously appropriate for the day after Christmas, it was certainly appropriate to Smith's situation in regard to his trial.

Smith begins by discussing the rights and wrongs of Jeroboam's rebellion against Rehoboam after the death of Solomon. The Puritan commentator Matthew Poole had argued that Jeroboam was wrong to rebel, because God had commanded that the Israelites should be loyal to David. Smith disagrees. God, in his revelation, never interferes with the natural laws of right and wrong, and there was much that was wrong with the dynasty of David. Solomon had imposed grievous burdens on the people, and God's promises to David were not a mandate for oppression. When Jeroboam rebelled he was sincerely trying to serve God. His rebellion was legitimate in that even David had had his rule over the northern tribes endorsed by them, while Rehoboam's journey to Shechem to meet the northern tribes implied that they had the right to accept or reject him. Jeroboam's revolt was accomplished without bloodshed and with the support of the people. As we reflect on this part of the sermon we are bound to ask whether both Smith and his hearers made connections between the rebellion and the Disruption of 1843.

There is also in this first section an anticipation of what Smith would say so powerfully in the public lectures given in January to March 1881 and published as *The Old Testament in the Jewish Church*.[22] In support of Jeroboam, Smith pointed out that the sanctuaries of Bethel and Dan were sanctuaries of Jehovah, and that Jeroboam was doing nothing wrong in breaking allegiance from Jerusalem. In fact, there were many

21. K1.
22. See p. 170.

legitimate sanctuaries. Elijah had complained to God that the people had broken down his altars. Further, there were bull images in the Jerusalem temple. Jeroboam did not try to introduce a new religion; he recalled his people to the old faith: 'Behold thy God, O Israel, which brought thee up out of the land of Egypt (1 Kgs 12.28)'. How, then, did Jeroboam go wrong? Not by any daring act of defiance against God but by an act of self-deception to which we can also succumb. Jeroboam had received a sacred trust, and that trust was Israel, 'set among the nations as the depository of God's revelation, as the guardian of the true knowledge of the eternal spiritual redeeming God'. However, 'the leaven of worldly purpose began to taint his profession of worship to Jehovah'. He wanted to emulate the temple in Jerusalem, and he thus set up an image at Bethel, in direct breach of the Ten Commandments.[23] He probably thought that this was only a small breach of the law—after all, had there not been an image in Dan since the days of the Judges? However, the effect of Jeroboam's action was fatal. It hastened the process of the 'national obliteration of the contrast between Jehovah and idols, till all true knowledge of God perished out of the land'. We notice here a further anticipation of *The Old Testament in the Jewish Church* as well as echoes of Smith's article on 'Bible' and 'Decalogue' in the *Encyclopaedia Britannica*.[24]

At this point in the sermon, Smith is able to point a lesson to the hearers:

> As Jeroboam yielded so we are apt to yield; by fancying that if our religious zeal is great, we shall be excused for mingling with it a grain of worldly purpose; by catching at convenient religious practices without bringing them to the test of God's word; and by thinking that it is our business instead of God's to take heed that his service do not hinder us in our lawful calling.

23. This seems to contradict what Smith says here and elsewhere in the sermon, when he points out that there were bull images in the Jerusalem temple. Today's reader naturally asks whether, for Smith, these images were a violation of the Ten Commandments. If they were, then Smith was inconsistent in justifying Jeroboam's general behaviour by saying that there were images in the Jerusalem temple and then condemning him in particular for setting up images at Dan and Bethel. If they were not, Smith had no case. This is a very rare instance of an apparent inconsistency in Smith's work.

24. See p. 174.

But if Jeroboam fell into error, he was given a chance by God to turn back. A prophet was sent to warn him, and when Jeroboam invited him to his home, Smith does not doubt

> that he was touched with some sense of danger if not of guilt and was anxious to have the counsel and support of so great a prophet in retracing his steps and forming some plan of amendment.

However, the prophet had no commission other than to warn Jeroboam; Jeroboam alone had to take the decision to go on or turn back.

The same was true of the prophet: he had a commission to fulfil, and that included neither eating nor drinking nor retracing his steps. However, he allowed his mind to be made up for him by another prophet, disobeyed his commission, and was later killed by a lion. There was a lesson here for Christians to be steadfast in obeying their own consciences:

> One great Church of professing Chistians has made it a matter of principle to yield up the right of private judgment in affairs of conscience into the hands of the priesthood. And we who are Protestants are not always free from the same bondage...we are all at some time ready to let another tell us what we shall believe and what we shall do without using for ourselves the test of the word and of conscience.

However, we are surely not mistaken in hearing in these last words something of Smith's own conviction that in the matters concerning his trial it was his duty to stand firm in what he believed to be the truth. The following words are similarly suggestive:

> Are you living in doubt of what God would have you do? Then commit not yourself to another man's reading of the divine will but be fully persuaded in your own mind. Take what counsel you may but follow no counsel that does not approve itself by the standard of the Word and commend itself to your conscience. And let your questioning of Word and conscience be a prayerful questioning that so the decision may be between you and God directly.

Smith ended the sermon by appealing to the example of Jesus. When we face up to our responsibilities and stand alone we are following Christ's example. He rejected the views of his disciples that suffering and death had no place in the work of the messiah; yet by standing alone he won a victory, and that victory is a pledge of our victory. Unusually for one of his sermons, Smith ended with a mosaic of biblical quotations, of which the last was from Rev. 3.21: 'To him that overcometh will I grant to sit with me in my throne, even as I also overcame, and am set down with my Father in his throne'. However, the penultimate quotation was from Isa. 43.2, a text on which Smith preached one of his most moving sermons.

The sermon on Isa. 43.1-2 was written in 1877, and thus at the beginning of the trial period, and was used at a communion service at East Church (Aberdeen) and also at a similar service in Buckie in 1880.[25] No doubt the context of the communion service affected the simple, direct and personal tone of the address. Nonetheless, the simple piety of Smith shines through it, and no one could possibly believe that it was not utterly sincere.

Isa. 43.1-2 reads as follows:

> But now thus saith the LORD that created thee, O Jacob, and he that formed thee, O Israel, Fear not: for I have redeemed thee, I have called thee by name; thou art mine. When thou passest through the waters, I will be with thee; and through the rivers, they shall not overflow thee: when thou walkest through the fire, thou shalt not be burned; neither shall the flame kindle upon thee.

The sermon is a straightforward, even literalist direct appropration of the promises in the passage to Smith and his hearers. But he sets the scene by referring back to Isa. 42.19: 'Who is blind, but my servant? or deaf, as my messenger that I sent?'

Smith describes the feelings with which worshippers may approach the communion table, feelings which concentrate upon human problems and concerns rather than the things of God:

> When we come to the communion table it is not always God's voice of grace that sounds most loudly in our ears. That voice is clear and strong and the Christ stands before us in full view in his own ordinance. But our ears are dull and our eyes dim and even the glorious sound and light of the gospel fall dead on them...Great things have been given to us to see and hear, and just on that account, just because God has done such things for us and we have been as unworthy of them we cannot but judge ourselves blind and deaf even beyond those who are outside the gospel pale.

Having thus sensitively outlined the possible mood of inadequacy felt by the worshippers as they approached communion, Smith draws out the promises in the text. It is 'the Lord that created thee who speaks, who has done marvellous things, who, in Christ has re-created us

25. K10.

through the word of the gospel (2 Cor. 5.17)'. But Smith makes most effective use of the words 'I have called thee by thy name'. He links this with the individual receiving of bread and wine in the communion, as well as with notable stories in the New Testament where Jesus deals with individuals. The following quotations indicate the force of the approach:

> I call thee by thy *name* thou art mine. I call thee by thy *name*. Not as one of the crowd merely. Jesus seeks thee out and puts his broken body and shed blood personally into thy very hands. I *call thee* by name. As of old he called Zacchaeus. Are we not standing today at the empty sepulchre as Mary stood unable to recognise a living Lord—Well! the word comes to us with as thrilling personal a call of life as it came to her. 'Jesus saith unto her, Mary. She turned..and saith unto him, Rabboni/Master.' Shall we not say Rabboni?

And Smith ended the pre-communion sermon with a prayer that skilfully combined the text with a traditional formula used when about to receive communion:

> Hear! for there is another word. Thou art *mine*...I am thine O Jesus. Abide this day in my house—I am not worthy that thou shouldest come under my roof.

It is now time to review this attempt to outline the typical content of Smith's sermons. His biographers commented, as we have seen, that Smith said nothing in his sermons that could have not have been heard from any orthodox Scottish preacher; and I presume that they had far more experience of listening to nineteenth-century Scottish preachers than I can have had! However, I must venture to disagree with Smith's biographers. Only Smith could have preached the sermon on Jeroboam's revolt, embodying as it did the critical view of the history of Israelite religion that cost him his job. Again, if I am right in seeing the influence of Albrecht Ritschl's view of the kingdom of God on Smith's sermons on that subject, we are *not* dealing with something that could have been said by any orthodox Scottish preacher. Smith, as a preacher, was probably much more original than his biographers allow, and it is probable that the low evaluation of Smith's preaching by the biographers has affected subsequent research on Smith.[26]

---

26. It is also worth repeating what was said in n. 14 above. In contrast to orthodox Scottish preachers, Smith did not once preach about the vicarious or expiatory benefits of Christ's death; and we must remember that he saw the essence of sacrifice in the Old Testament in terms of communion, not propitiation. In this regard, Smith's

Smith's sermons are important for several reasons. First, they provide evidence for the development of his critical views by indicating that, in 1870–1872, he was prepared to ascribe Psalms such as Psalm 32 to David and Psalm 90 to Moses. Secondly, they indicate the stability of his basic Christian convictions during the period 1872–1880 when his critical views were developing rapidly. There are two sermons that he preached a total of 42 times between 1871 and 1881 that support this conclusion strongly.

Thirdly, and most importantly, the sermons are the most direct route to Smith the man of faith. They show us a side that we might not suspect of the man who independently embraced critical positions also advocated by Kuenen and Wellhausen, and who argued that Israelite tribes had once borne the animal names of the totems that they worshipped. The sermons reveal a Smith who believed that Jesus had called him personally to the service of his kingdom, a kingdom that had been established by Christ's death and which, through the power of Christ's love, was destined to incorporate and sum up all that was best in human labour, knowledge and service. The service of the kingdom was not an appendage to human plans or ambitions; it was the all-embracing service which was perfect freedom. The history of grace, recorded in the Bible, proclaimed the kingdom, enabled entry and sustained its servants.

Smith stopped preaching after his dismissal in 1881. His clerical status had been linked to his chair, and he judged that they went together.[27] During his Cambridge exile he confided that, if the Presbyterian congregation in Cambridge were to be provided with a regular minister with whom he could feel at ease, he would be glad to assist the congregation by giving lectures on the Bible.[28] It seems that he never lost his attachment to ministering to congregations. Perhaps one of the effects of his dismissal was to deprive us of more sermons which, if published, may have ranked him among the notable preachers of the nineteenth century.

scholarly and homiletical views seem to have been identical.

27. Black and Chrystal (*Life of William Robertson Smith*, pp. 461-62) note that the year after his dismissal from his Free Church Chair, he attended the General Assembly as a lay elder.

28. Smith to a friend (see n. 1 p. 130 above), M10, p. 12.

Chapter 9

SMITH IN RETROSPECT

When, early in 1894, it became apparent to William Robertson Smith that he did not have long to live, he confided two regrets to his friend Thomas Lindsay. To quote Lindsay:

> he desired to outlive his mother, whose grief at his death would be overwhelming, and he longed to spare her that sorrow; and he was very anxious to finish his Burnett Lectures. He recurred to those unfinished Lectures several times, and always with one dominant idea...he longed to be able 'to complete his argument'.[1]

The Burnett Lectures referred to were the lectures delivered in Aberdeen from 1888 to 1891, of which only the first series was published, and of which the second and third series were not worked into a form suitable for publication (although they will now be published in an edited version by John Day in 1995). But what was the argument that Smith longed to be able to complete?

Another account of the dying Smith's words to his friend Lindsay, given by John F. White, reads as follows:

> I should like to live a little longer for two things—to survive my mother that she may not have the pain of hearing of my death, and next, that I may finish my book in which I intend to show to the world the Divine Revelation of God in the Old Testament.[2]

There can be no doubt that the two versions of Smith's dying wishes refer to the same thing. The 'book' is almost certainly the second and third series of Burnett Lectures, and the argument is an argument about what Smith believed to be the unique value of the Bible as divine revelation. Smith believed that if the Old Testament were compared with the religion of other ancient Semitic peoples, the superiority of Israelite

1. Black and Chrystal, *Life of William Robertson Smith*, p. 550.
2. White, *Two Professors of Oriental Languages*, p. 34.

religion would be clear for all to see, and that it would be possible to draw the conclusion that this superiority could not have been a human achievement, but was made possible only by the self-revealing activity of God.

Towards the end of the last series of Burnett Lectures there survives a passage which is written out in full, and which is partly quoted by Smith's biographers.[3] It deserves to be given in full, however, with the explanation that it concludes a lecture in which Smith compared the narratives of Genesis, especially the creation stories, with the recently-discovered texts from Babylonia. Smith wrote:

> The Hebrew stories in Genesis, looked at in their plain sense, contain much that is *not* directly edifying. They do not make the patriarchs models of goodness but they never make religion involve the approbation of a lower morality or a low view of the deity. In them God communes with men without ever lowering himself to the level of man; He has no human passions or affections, for his love of his chosen people is raised far above the weaknesses of human preferences. Above all, he is the God of the world before he is Israel's God; while in all the Semitic legends the Demiurge himself is always, and above all, the local King.
>
> The burden of explaining this contrast does not lie with us; it falls on those who are compelled by a false philosophy of revelation to see in the Old Testament nothing more than the highest tendencies of Semitic religion. That is not the view that study commends to me. It is a view that is not commended but condemned by the many parallelisms in detail between Hebrew and heathen story and ritual. For all these material points of resemblance only make the contrast in spirit more remarkable.[4]

These words from the final series of Burnett Lectures, together with Smith's sentiments expressed to Lindsay about wanting to live long enough to complete his argument, are important evidence in support of the view that, however some of Smith's opinions may have changed during his lifetime, what did not change was his belief in the Old Testament as a divine revelation. Nor did he give up the belief that he had a vocation to demonstrate to the learned world of his day that the Old Testament contained a unique revelation.

It is necessary to stress this point because attempts have been made to argue otherwise. For example, Warner Bailey, in his unpublished Yale

---

3. Black and Chrystal, *Life of William Robertson Smith*, pp. 536-37.

4. Cambridge University Library ADD 7476 H76. This extract is not from the last of the Burnett Lectures, as Black and Chrystal imply; it is from the third lecture of the Third Series.

dissertation, traces the correspondence between Smith and Kuenen from 1880 to 1882 and points out what he believes to be a progressive movement towards Kuenen's views.[5]

Another comment, which needs to be evaluated carefully, comes from the biographical sketch published in 1903 by James Bryce. Commenting on the Burnett Lectures Bryce wrote:

> Only the first volume was published, for death overtook the author before he could put into final shape the materials he had collected for the full development of his theories. As the second volume would have traced the connection between the primitive religion of the Arab branches of the Semitic stock (including Israel) and the Hebrew religion as we have it in the earlier books of the Old Testament, the absence of this finished statement is a loss to science. Changes had passed upon his views since he wrote the incriminated articles, and he said to me (I think about 1888) that

---

5.　　W.M. Bailey, 'Theology and Criticism in William Robertson Smith' (PhD dissertation, Yale University, 1970). Bailey's careful and well-modulated discussion concerns Kuenen's doubts about how it was possible for Smith to combine faith and criticism in the way that he did, and Smith's reactions to Kuenen's observations. Bailey draws particular attention to Smith's words in a letter dated 26 August 1882, written after Smith had read Kuenen's Hibbert Lectures, published as *National Religions and Universal Religions* (London, 1882). Part of the extract reads 'To me personally it has been very pleasing, because it satisfies me more than ever that there is far less difference between my super-naturalism and yours than I once thought or than most people here think still; and this makes me more confident that what I have learned from you as a critic is not inconsistent with the faith I still hold. I do not think that any one need ask a higher prerogative for Christianity than that in it the right line of evolution of the true knowledge of God can be traced continuously without those interruptions and even doubling back that are seen in other universal religions.'

Some of Bailey's most important conclusions are summed up as follows (pp. 292-93): 'in his *Prophets*, 1882, and in his 1882 letter to Kuenen, Smith does not retain in view the possibility of the inner testimony of the Holy Spirit as the verifier of the Knowledge of God. Furthermore the definition of Scripture has changed. Before his trial and in the first edition of the *OTJC*, Smith had argued that historical criticism arises out of an interest in biblical history because it is a history of address and response. This evangelical thrust has been greatly attenuated in his *Prophets*, 1882, and has been lost in his 1882 letter to Kuenen, to be replaced in both cases by a theoretical argument of the invincible arguments of truth.'

Bailey's argument deserves discussion in a full-length article. I would simply point out in defence of the position presented in these lectures that Smith did not alter his account of the importance of historical criticism in the 1892 edition of *The Old Testament in the Jewish Church*, and that he repeated some of his earlier views on prophecy in the second and third series of Burnett Lectures. See Chapter 7 above.

he would no longer undertake any clerical duties. He had a sensitive conscience, and held that no clergyman ought to use language in the pulpit which did not express his personal convictions.[6]

These last two sentences could be read as though Smith had given up Christian faith, or had ceased to be orthodox. Both conclusions would be mistaken. We have evidence that Smith earnestly hoped that the Presbyterian congregation meeting in Cambridge would get a minister with whom he would feel at ease; in which case Smith would join the congregation and would offer to give classes on the Bible to the congregation.[7] My own reading of Bryce's account is that Smith felt that his views on biblical criticism would be too radical to be voiced in a pulpit and that he would be unhappy, for example, to imply to a congregation that they were about to use a psalm of David, when Smith dated Davidic psalms about 600 years later than Israel's poet king.

Let us grant the truth of what I have been arguing in these lectures: that Smith developed, and throughout his life maintained, a theological position that made him at one and the same time a leading and some-times radical biblical critic, and a fervent evangelical committed to bringing human knowledge under the lordship of Christ. Let us grant this, and ask what we make of him a hundred years after his death. I intend to consider three matters: first, his view of history as containing a divine revelation, secondly, his biblical critical views in the light of modern scholarship, and thirdly, his pleas for a believing criticism of the Bible.

Of all Smith's convictions, the one that I find most problematic is his view that history contains a divine revelation.[8] Yet to criticize Smith on this score is to criticize many of the leading thinkers of the nineteenth century; and not only thinkers of the nineteenth but the twentieth century also. Nobody who was in touch with the intellectual currents of thought in nineteenth-century Europe could have remained unaffected by the view that history could have meaning, and Smith was no

6. J. Bryce, *Studies in Contemporary Biography* (New York: Macmillan, 1903), p. 321.

7. Reminiscence of a friend, Cambridge University Library ADD 7476 M 10, p. 12. Also to be noted is the evidence in Black and Chrystal, *Life of William Robertson Smith*, pp. 461-62, that Smith linked his clerical status with his College post, and appeared at the General Assembly the year after his dismissal as a lay elder.

8. To be more accurate, I should say that Smith believed that it was through historical processes that God revealed himself to Israel, not forgetting the interpretative function of the prophets, whose personal relationship to God was an important factor.

exception. There is no need to look for specific influences here; they are all-pervasive. Not only were there the idealist and materialist versions of history as an unfolding and dialectical process, views popularly associated with Hegel and Marx respectively. Other philosophers, such as Schelling, saw history as an unfolding intrusion into human affairs of a supernatural dialectic; and these various philosophies were taken up into the work of professional historians and Old Testament scholars such as Niebuhr and Ewald, and even into the theologies of conservative German theologians such as von Hofmann and Delitzsch.[9] Among scholars who must have influenced Smith or whom he had read, and who held views of history similar to those he embraced, we can list Bunsen, Rothe, Delitzsch, Ewald and von Hofmann. Further, we must not forget that similar views of history, probably arriving from Germany via Niebuhr and Bunsen, had established themselves in British thought, and had been expressed by Milman in his *History of the Jews*, by Thomas Arnold in his sermons, and by Frederick Temple in his essay on the Education of the World in *Essays and Reviews*.[10]

We who live in an age separated from Smith's by two World Wars, and by a century that has seen the most inhumane treatment of human beings, and of the other species that inhabit the earth, that has ever been devised, will find it hard to understand the wonderful optimism that must have characterized Smith's times and emboldened him to see history in such a positive way. Speaking personally, I feel about history as I feel about nature, when the design of nature is appealed to in support of the existence of God. Although I can be moved to awe and admiration by the sublimity of waterfalls, landscapes, seascapes and individual flowers, I can never overlook the pain and suffering that are endemic in the world of nature. If nature proclaims that it has a creator, I am not at all sure that I like, or want to have to do with, the creator that is implied—a creator that seems either to be cruel, or indifferent to cruelty. I find myself in sympathy with the observations that may or may not have been written by Nietzsche, which see in nature nothing other than a will to power.[11]

9.   See Rogerson, *Old Testament Criticism*, esp. chs. 6–8.
10.   *Old Testament Criticism*, ch. 13.
11.   As is well known, Nietzsche left only a series of fragments and sketches of a book about the will to power, and the work of that name was put together after his death. See *Friedrich Nietzsche, Sämtliche Werke* (eds. G. Collic and M. Montinari; Munich: DTV; Berlin: de Gruyter, 1980), XIV, pp. 381-400.

I feel the same about history. I accept that the claim can be made that the coming of Christ into the world coincided with world conditions—the spread of the Greek language as a kind of vernacular and the existence of the Roman Empire in one of its more peaceful phases—that were ideal for the spread of Christianity, and that were therefore providential. But the awful conditions that followed the end of the First World War were also ideal for the rise of a monster such as Hitler, and the technological advances of modern warfare and mass extermination were as favourable to his plans for the human race as was the Pax Romana for the spread of Christianity. History can be seen in terms of the will to power just as much as nature.

But there is a further fundamental question, which is whether there is such a thing as history or whether there are only histories (or herstories, as some feminists would have it). This is not a question that has been prompted by postmodernism, although postmodernism has given it a new dimension. I have in mind the questions raised by works such as A.C. Danto's *An Analytical Philosophy of History* and Hans Michael Baumgartner's *Kontinuität und Geschichte*; the latter concentrates upon the extent to which what are regarded as connections and continuities in history are in fact interpretations provided by participators, observers and writers of history.[12] The whole picture has subsequently been made more complicated by the postmodern questionings of the possibility of objectivity in history writing. Personally, I take these discussions seriously to the point of accepting that our access to the past can only be by way of narrative, that any narrative is essentially an art form, and that narratives are shaped by special interests both when they are written and when they are read. On the other hand, this does not entail that histories are simply *invented* by human beings, and that there is no need to do historical research. In preparing these lectures on Smith, I have done a great deal of historical research and have discovered things whose existence I had not suspected. At the same time I am conscious that my use of this historical research is inevitably shaped by my particular interests.

12. A.C. Danto, *An Analytical Philosophy of History* (Cambridge: Cambridge University Press, 1965); H.M. Baumgartner, *Kontinuität und Geschichte: Zur Kritik und Metakritik der historischen Vernunft* (Frankfurt: Suhrkamp, 1972). See further my article 'Is there a Doctrine of Providence in the Old Testament?', in L. Esslinger *et al.* (eds.), *Ascribe to the Lord: Essays in Memory of Peter C. Craigie* (JSOTSup, 67; Sheffield: JSOT Press, 1988), pp. 529-43.

How does this affect our assessment of Smith? By using source criticism Smith dismantled the Old Testament's own understanding of its history of religion and sacrifice, and reassembled it into what he believed the actual history had been.[13] His action was, and remains, a legitimate exercise within biblical studies. But as an apologist for Christianity, Smith, in doing this, became a hostage to fortune in several ways. First, he opened up the possibility that subsequent research would find objections to the reconstructed history that he embraced, and would propose alternative reconstructions that might even militate against seeing in Israel's history a history of God's grace. My suspicion is that Smith would have allowed this as a possibility, but would have thought such a development to be unlikely. The sense of discovery that the new reconstruction of Israel's literary and religious history brought in the second part of the nineteenth century must have made the scholars of Smith's generation, and of the next couple of generations, feel that they had arrived at a sure result that would never be challenged.

Secondly, Smith became vulnerable to objections to his notion of history, and to the divine revelation that he saw within it. Obviously, he could have had no idea that later scholarship would question whether there is such a thing as history as an objective process that scholars can describe or reconstruct. He could have had no inkling that there would be calls for Israel's history to be rewritten so as to recover the stories of the women and the oppressed classes that a male-dominated ruling class had suppressed or ignored in the production of the Old Testament. But such calls are a feature of the 1990s, and they cannot be ignored when Smith is being evaluated today. Thirdly, by claiming or implying that his reconstructed version of Israelite history was a history of grace, Smith was substituting a human authority for the authority of the Bible. I do not blame him for doing this, since he was not alone in his own day, nor in the preceding or following generations. But it is one thing to say that the Bible is the record of a revelation, and quite another thing to use the Bible simply as evidence along with other evidence, such as that from archaeology, to reconstruct a history of revelation that can always be open to challenge and modification. That Smith felt able to do this resulted from his belief, shared with his contemporaries, that history was an objective process in which God was at work and which could be

13. He made the further assumption that this *reconstructed* history was *objective* history in which God's guidance of Israel could be seen.

reconstructed with reasonable certainty by the new methods of historical criticism.

Can we salvage anything from what may seem to be the wreckage of this part of Smith's position? We could fight a rearguard action against the newer ideas of the nature of history, rather as Pannenberg does, and object to the secularization of the notion of history and to the banishment of God from the world that this secularization implies.[14] A more realistic approach, and one informed by some of Smith's insights, would go as follows. Smith always stresses that what was learnt in Israel about the nature and will of God was learnt by struggle. This was especially true of the prophets, who found themselves in conflict with the rulers of Israel and Judah, with the rich and powerful, and with the common people. Their contribution to Israel's faith was to proclaim, in the particular circumstances in which they found themselves, the implications of belief in God, who was a God of justice and of liberation. They came into conflict with their nation especially when they saw the national interest not in terms of political survival of the nation at all costs, but in terms of the vocation of the nation as a witness to God's justice.

By developing this point, we can say that the importance of the prophets lay in their witness—a witness to an aspect of reality that was not apparent to most of their contemporaries; a witness that had the power to help the nation overcome major disasters such as the destruction of Jerusalem in 587–586 and to reconstitute the nation as a people with a vocation. But this witness also exerted a powerful influence on the way in which Israel's story was reinterpreted and re-written in the post-exilic period. This is particularly striking in the case of the story of Moses; for this story of Israel's founding hero is almost a tragedy, as Moses is rejected by the people he has brought out of slavery, is plotted against by members of his own family, and is finally excluded by God from the promised land because he belongs to the generation which, although freed from slavery, has shown itself to be unfit to carry God's plan to the next stage. It is possible to make similar observations about the story of Jeremiah.

What this leads to is a reinstating of the text of the Old Testament as the locus of revelation, as opposed to locating the revelation in the history that Smith and others reconstructed with the help of the Old Testament. But the reinstating of the text is not a return to the literalism

14. See W. Pannenberg, 'Geschichte', VIII, 5, in *TRE*, XII (1984), pp. 667ff.

that Smith rejected. It is not a return to the view that the text is revelation rather than the record of a revelation. What we might call a hermeneutics of witness, or of testimony, is closer to Smith's view that the Bible is the record of a revelation than it is to the literalist view. What it amounts to saying, in line with narrative and postmodern views of history, is that the Old Testament contains histories which, in their interpretative thrusts, articulate a witness to a God who was believed to have liberated Israel from slavery, but whose purposes transcended the national interest of that people, and made claims to universal sovereignty for the purposes of establishing justice and peace among all peoples. This witness further articulates what we might call the cost of discipleship, as it presents the story of the people and of some of its religious teachers in terms of suffering, misunderstanding and rejection.

Our difference from Smith is that he was able to dismantle the Old Testament's story of Israel, and to reassemble it in a form that he believed represented the actual history of God's dealings with his people. We, today, are similarly committed as academics to probing behind the Old Testament's own story in an attempt to discover what was happening in ancient Israel from the twelfth century BCE onwards. But we cannot, if we are also theologians, expect our reconstructions to be a history of God's grace. They are simply *our* reconstructions, open to falsification or modification, and, in accordance with postmodern sensitivities, concerned with women, slaves, the oppressed classes and popular religion and not simply with the fate of kings, priests and official religion. It we are theologians we must go back to the witness to faith that the Old Testament stories articulate, noting their remarkable self-criticism and their stress on the suffering aspects of discipleship, among other things. If, with Smith, we want to claim that this witness is unique in the context of the other religions of the ancient Near East, and is no mere human achievement, this is something that, as theologians, we are entitled to do, and which we must be prepared to defend, as Smith did in his Burnett Lectures.

I come now to the second matter of this lecture, the issue of how the critical positions that Smith adopted compare with the views of subsequent scholarship. I begin with the so-called Wellhausen view of Israel's literature and religion, where subsequent scholarship can be summarized in terms of three main phases: initial widespread acceptance, growing rejection, and reacceptance and beyond to positions even more radical than the 'Wellhausen position'. Of the initial widespread acceptance, to which Smith's *The Old Testament in the Jewish Church* contributed greatly in Britain, little needs to be said.[15] The reaction against the 'Wellhausen position' was inspired by Palestinian archaeology and the discoveries of ancient Near Eastern texts, and was led particularly from America but with some support from Germany, Britain and Scandinavia.

Already in his lifetime, Wellhausen was accused of ignoring recently-discovered Assyrian and Babylonian texts (the same charge was made—unfairly—against Smith), and certainly one of the main thrusts of scholars upholding the traditional view of Israel's history and religion at the end of the nineteenth century was that the newly-discovered texts and monuments confirmed the accuracy of the Old Testament.[16] In the twentieth century this view was propagated by the so-called Albright school, which pioneered Palestinian archaeology and which apparently displayed a conservative desire to defend the basic historicity of the Bible.[17] Further, at least one member of the Albright school, G.E. Wright, envisaged the task of biblical theology as being to reconstruct the mighty and revelatory acts of God in history by means of the Bible and archaeological discoveries.[18] In Germany, the (relatively) conservative Leipzig scholar Albrecht Alt used archaeological discoveries to sketch the profile of the kind of religious founders that Abraham and Isaac and Jacob might have been.[19] Certainly, when I became a student in 1957 the book described as 'modern biblical scholarship at its best' was G.E. Wright's *Biblical Archaeology*, a book which gave a very reassuring and traditional account of Israelite history and religion, from the time of Abraham onwards;[20] and this was followed up in 1961 by John Bright's *A History of Israel*, which again followed a traditional line

15. See my lecture on *The Old Testament in the Jewish Church*, pp. 177-78 below.

16. For the charge against Wellhausen see my *Anthropology and the Old Testament* (Biblical Seminar, 1; repr.; Sheffield: JSOT Press, 1984 [1978]), p. 30. Scholars who held that the monuments and the like confirmed the traditional version of the Old Testament history included G. Rawlinson, A.H. Sayce and, in Germany, the earlier work of R. Kittel.

17. See, for example, W.F. Albright's *From the Stone Age to Christianity* (Garden City, NY: Doubleday, 2nd edn, 1957).

18. G.E. Wright, *God Who Acts: Biblical Theology as Recital* (SBT, 8; London: SCM Press, 1952).

19. A. Alt, 'Der Gott der Väter', in *Kleine Schriften zur Geschichte des Volkes Israel* (Munich: Beck, 1959), I, pp. 1-78.

20. G.E. Wright, *Biblical Archaeology* (London: Duckworth; Philadelphia: Westminster Press, 2nd edn, 1962).

while making frequent reference to archaeological discoveries.[21]

Today the situation has altered radically. While defenders of a more traditional approach can still be found, there is a new radicalism abroad which not only doubts whether Abraham, Jacob or Moses ever existed, but which questions whether David and Solomon were any more real than the legendary King Arthur.[22] There is an increasing tendency to date all the main sources of the Pentateuch—J, E and P—to the post-exilic period and to be sceptical about how much can be known of the history of Judah and Israel before the exile. My own view of these developments is that, in many cases, they go too far. But I also have no doubt that a consensus will emerge in a few years that sees the eighth century (the time of Hezekiah) rather than the tenth century (the time of David and Solomon) as the most formative period in the development of a consciousness of Israel as a special nation apart from its neighbours.

The study of the Psalms, another matter of importance to Smith, has witnessed a similar cycle to that of the history of Israel and its religion. Whereas in the second edition of *The Old Testament in the Jewish Church* in 1892 Smith dated all the psalms in the period roughly 450–160 BCE, the early twentieth century witnessed a determined attempt to reinstate as many psalms as possible in the pre-exilic period. The scholars particularly associated with this movement were Gunkel and Mowinckel, and their reasons for suggesting earlier datings are of importance to any consideration of Smith.[23] Whereas Smith had seen the Psalms as expressing the piety of the official worship and of individuals of the Second Temple, Mowinckel and his followers stressed the symbolic function of psalms in the life of the community. Basing their claims upon Babylonian examples, they argued that annual or periodic rituals took place in the First Temple in which the king played a central role, prob-ably undergoing ritual humiliation, death, resurrection and even possibly sacred marriage in order to ensure the well-being of the nation and the fertility of its land and animals.[24] This approach to the Psalms was

21. J. Bright, *A History of Israel* (London: SCM Press, 1961). Subsequent editions did not materially alter the conclusions, although the footnotes were updated and the text revised in some instances.

22. An excellent statement of this type of approach is given by P.R. Davies, *In Search of Ancient Israel* (JSOTSup, 148; Sheffield: JSOT Press, 1992).

23. See H. Gunkel's *Die Psalmen übersetzt und erklärt* (HAT; Göttingen: Vandenhoeck & Ruprecht, 4th edn, 1926) and S. Mowinckel's *The Psalms in Israel's Worship* (trans. D.R. Ap-Thomas; Oxford: Basil Blackwell, 1962).

24. For more on this approach generally, see my *Myth in Old Testament*

pressed into service as a source of Israelite belief in the universal sovereignty of the God of Israel, and of the hope for the eschatological Day of the Lord when that divine sovereignty would become a universal reality. In other words, whereas Smith had dated the Psalms late and had seen them as expressing a distinctive Israelite piety, this new research dated them early, and looked to Babylon as the source for the main thrusts of Israelite religion. Again, when I became a student in 1957, a book that was strongly recommended and that articulated this kind of approach was A.R. Johnson's *Sacral Kingship in Ancient Israel*.[25]

Today, there seems to be a swinging back to the late dating of the Psalms, along with the general trend to date Old Testament literature in the post-exilic period.[26] In other words, things are returning closer to where they were at the time of Smith's death.

If this is true of the Psalms, however, it is not true of the prophetic literature, which was so important to Smith. Whereas Smith saw the prophets as inspired individuals who stood against the stream of their contemporaries and who directed the gaze of the nation away from its own interests to those of a transcendent deity, recent scholarship has studied the prophets sociologically.[27] They have been called 'intermediaries' and have been studied along with intermediaries in other cultures, including modern traditional cultures in Africa or North America. They have been investigated in the light of role theory. Emphasis has been put upon their support groups, the expectations of these support groups, and the interplay between a prophet and the support group. The Old Testament prophets have been classified in terms of two main different types: central morality prophets—figures such as Isaiah who were close to the establishment and who supported it at times of crisis such as Sennacherib's invasion in 701 BCE; and peripheral, amoral prophets—figures such as Elijah who constantly challenged the establishment and some of whose actions, such as destroying pursuers

Interpretation (BZAW, 134; Berlin: de Gruyter, 1974), ch. 6.

25. A.R. Johnson, *Sacral Kingship in Ancient Israel* (Cardiff: University of Wales Press, 2nd edn, 1967).

26. See E. Gerstenberger, *Psalms, Part 1* (FOTL, 14; Grand Rapids: Eerdmans, 1988).

27. See particularly the works by R.R. Wilson, *Prophecy and Society in Ancient Israel* (Philadelphia: Fortress Press, 1980), and D. Petersen, *The Roles of Israel's Prophets* (JSOTSup, 17; Sheffield: JSOT Press, 1981).

by bringing down upon them fire from heaven, can best be described as amoral. An attempt has been made to see the prophets of the northern kingdom Israel as essentially different from those of the southern kingdom Judah, with the former being predominantly peripheral prophets and the latter being predominantly central morality prophets. Paradoxically, at the same time that the prophets have been studied sociologically, based upon the assumption that the prophets were actual people whose social setting and interactions can be described, another strand of Old Testament scholarship has suggested that the prophets as we have them in the literature are much more literary creations than has been previously appreciated, and that the recovery of their lives, times and social settings is far from easy.[28]

Before I ask what Smith would have made of these developments, I must comment that although the various sociological studies alluded to have thrown up interesting points, the theses that they have proposed have, in my opinion, often required the evidence to be used in ways that are far from convincing. Also, it is my view that we do not possess sufficient information about Israelite society in the period from 900 to 580 BCE to enable proper sociological studies to be carried out. However, the sociological approach must not be criticized or rejected on these grounds. It is always possible that new sociological models will enable Old Testament prophets to be described more convincingly in terms of the evidence available, and that new discoveries will fill in the gaps in our knowledge of Israelite society.

What, then, would Smith have made of these developments? Our first instinct would probably be to say that, as one who has come to be regarded as a founder of the sociological study of religion, Smith would have welcomed them. But if Smith had welcomed them (and let us assume this for the sake of the argument) he would also have had to find or propose a complementary approach that would have enabled him to see the prophets as men inspired by God. We must remind ourselves that whatever else he was, Smith was a theologian and an apologist for Christianity. We must not forget that, in dealing with prophecy, he sharply opposed the rationalist criticism which described the achievements of the prophets in purely human terms. Therefore, we can say that Smith would have welcomed sociological approaches to Old Testament prophets so long as he did not think that they were purely

---

28. See R.P. Carroll, *From Chaos to Covenant: Uses of Prophecy in the Book of Jeremiah* (London: SCM Press, 1981).

rationalist or reductionist, and provided that the divine inspiration of the prophets could still be described and defended. In my view, the best way to do this would be to concentrate upon the prophetic literature of the Old Testament, and to say that this literature contains a *witness* to the divine word believed to have been given to the prophets. This brings me to the final matter of this lecture, which concerns Smith's advocacy of a believing criticism.

The view that religious belief is not only out of place in academic studies, but is also an aberration, is not new.[29] In an article on Smith published soon after his death in the *Free Review*, the anonymous author wondered how it was possible that Smith 'pursued the methods of rationalistic literary analysis while holding the faith of Bibliolatrous superstition'.[30] What caused 'that strange hiatus or collapse of judgement' that enabled a man whose outstanding intellectual powers were acknowledged by all who knew him to believe in the divine inspiration of the Hebrew and Christian sacred books?

> How came he, after realising that not only Biblical literature as a whole but nearly every ostensibly homogeneous section is a structure of various and divergent hands, plans, times, ideals—how came he still to think that these composites are products of 'revelation' and 'inspiration' in a sense which no other extra-Christian literature is?[31]

The writer's answer to these and other shrewdly expressed paradoxes of Smith's position was that Smith's enormous intellectual energy was devoted to activities such as 'mathematics, languages, problems of detail, of words, of texts, of styles'; and that these exertions allowed little opportunity for philosophical depth or penetrating and original judgment. Even Smith's appearance bore this out:

> witness the fullness of the lower eyelid and the outer end of the eyebrow in his portrait: but his head does not suggest profundity; and his immense textual erudition almost excluded it.[32]

29. In fact, it goes back at least to the eighteenth century, and resurfaces from time to time in various forms. In Smith's day, his friend Kuenen was convinced that criticism and traditional faith were mutually exclusive, although he admired the honest way in which Smith tried to combine the two. There is a good treatment in Bailey, *Theology and Criticism*, pp. 266ff.

30. 'Scotulus', 'Professor Robertson Smith: A Problem', in *The Free Review* 2.2 (May 1894), pp. 97-98.

31. 'A Problem', p. 99.

32. 'A Problem', p. 103.

Smith, along with J.H. Newman and Pascal, was dismissed as someone who was restricted by prejudice in matters outside his field of competence, and who functioned rationally with only part of his intellect.

Today, the charge might be put differently, but no less damagingly, by saying that, in academic study of the Bible, religious commitment may distort a scholar's approach to scientific matters, and that while an individual scholar is entitled to believe that the Bible is inspired, that conviction should play no part in that scholar's academic work. In other words, there is no place for Smith's 'believing criticism', in a university at any rate.

Smith might have responded to these views as follows. First, he would have rejected any implication that it was in order to practise believing criticism in an ecclesiastical institution such as a seminary, but inappropriate to do so in an university. He himself worked in both, and while Professor of Arabic at Cambridge brought out a second edition of *The Old Testament in the Jewish Church* whose passionate defence of the Old Testament as a history of divine grace was repeated from the first edition. In any case, Smith would not have accepted that there were two kinds of truth, one for universities and another for theological seminaries. His stand on this had cost him his job in Aberdeen, and the last thing he wanted was for seminarians to be sheltered from new knowledge.[33]

Secondly, Smith would have agreed that if religious commitment prevented a scholar from accepting a critical position that seemed to be clearly demonstrated by the evidence, then that scholar's commitment was a hindrance to the truth. Smith's own willingness to alter his critical views in line with the evidence as he saw it supports this point.[34] Thirdly, Smith would have strongly insisted on the opposite point, namely, that an anti-religious commitment can prevent a scholar from accepting a critical position indicated by the evidence; and he would have developed this to the point where he would have insisted that just as believing critics could learn much from rationalist critics, so rationalists could learn much from believers.

This learning process for rationalists could work in two ways. First, a believer dealing with an essentially religious literature, literature including the language of prayer and worship, might well contribute insights borne of familiarity with prayer and worship. Secondly, in a believing scholar's

---

33. See his inaugural lecture at the Free Church College in November 1870, reprinted in *Lectures and Essays*, pp. 232-33.
34. See Chapter 6 above.

quest to articulate a Christian apologetic, information might be discovered that was of value to all scholars, whether believers or not. This second point is well exemplified in Smith's own life. It has been argued in these lectures that Smith determined to learn Arabic (he already had a formidable knowledge of Greek and Latin) so that he could study at first hand the sources of our knowledge of Semitic polytheism, and thereby compare that religion with what he believed to be the superior achievement of the Old Testament.[35] Whatever we may think about the project and its outcome, we cannot deny that Smith collected a great deal of data and that he formulated theories about it that affected subsequent scholarship, especially social anthropology and sociology. It is unlikely that anyone else could have done all this. To have banned Smith's project on academic grounds would have robbed academic studies of a major source of information.

From a postmodern perspective we must say that it is surely inadmissible to reject from the humanities in a university an approach that has a religious commitment. If, as I would argue, it is permissible to have a feminist commitment, or a materialist commitment, or a Freudian commitment within the humanities, how can the rejection of a religious commitment be justified? The humanities have gained a new lease of life by their openness to a plurality of approaches that could not have been envisaged forty years ago; and what is true of the humanities in general is true of the study of the Bible in particular. Forty years ago the historical-critical method was the all-sufficient method within biblical studies. Today it is one method, and an indispensable one, among a plurality of approaches that represent different interests. So long as these interests are clearly identified we gain by admitting them to the academy and lose by excluding any of them.

Smith took the position that he did not because he had an intellectual defect, as alleged by the article in the *Free Review*, but because he stood within a tradition of faith and commitment that went back to the beginnings of Christianity, and before that to the community of faith that produced the Old Testament. Smith's acceptance of that tradition was not second-hand. It was based upon wide-ranging philosophical, historical and theological studies which convinced Smith of the vitality of the tradition in a changing world. It was not simply an intellectual exercise but a commitment that embraced every aspect of life, and which was concerned with the advancement of the kingdom of God in

---

35. See above pp. 110-11.

human society. In the context of daily living, teaching, worship and preaching Smith found that the Bible spoke to his deepest needs and realistically expressed the sufferings and problems of those committed to God's kingdom in a world of human strife and wickedness. When his own church lost confidence in him he did not abandon the tradition, nourished as he had been by his contacts with German theology.

What Smith tried to do for his own day was to affirm and interpret that tradition of commitment which he had embraced, for a changing world and the implications of new knowledge. His achievement was remarkable. Without in any way compromising his belief that, in the Judeo-Christian Scriptures and believing communities, God had proclaimed and established a kingdom that was meant to draw all humanity together in voluntary acknowledgment of the truth, Smith entered into critical dialogue with the new knowledge, displaying a fearless openness to wherever the truth would lead. Without his contribution, the theological and intellectual worlds of his day would have been immeasurably poorer, as witness his work for the *Encyclopaedia Britannica*. His own life is the strongest argument for the importance of a believing criticism.

But that life ended in 1894 at the age of 47, and not in 1904 or 1914 at the age of 57 or 67. What he might have achieved had he enjoyed ten or twenty more years of active scholarship we can only speculate. What he actually achieved in a mere 47 years remains a source of wonderment and inspiration.

Part III

KEYNOTE ADDRESS TO W.R. SMITH CONGRESS, ABERDEEN,
APRIL 1994

Chapter 10

W.R. SMITH'S *THE OLD TESTAMENT IN THE JEWISH CHURCH*:
ITS ANTECEDENTS, ITS INFLUENCE AND ITS ABIDING VALUE

At the end of October 1880 a Commission of Assembly appointed to examine W.R. Smith's article 'Hebrew Language and Literature' in volume XI of the ninth edition of the *Encyclopaedia Britannica* voted by a majority of 68 votes to suspend him from his chair of Hebrew and Old Testament Exegesis at the Free Church College of Aberdeen.[1] Thus began an interlude of feverish activity of some seven months before Smith's second trial before the General Assembly in May 1881 and his dismissal. Part of this interlude, from January to March 1881, was devoted to giving public lectures in Glasgow and Edinburgh setting out his views on the Old Testament and its critical study, and these lectures were published in May 1881 under the title *The Old Testament in the Jewish Church*.[2] A second, revised and enlarged, edition appeared in 1892, and it is this edition that is best known and most widely available. I shall refer to it at the end of this lecture. My main attention will be devoted to the first edition, however, because it is a landmark in the history of biblical criticism in Britain, in particular because it laid before the general public the critical view to which Wellhausen had given classical expression in his *Geschichte Israels* which had appeared less than three years earlier, in 1878.[3]

Wellhausen's account of the history of ancient Israelite religion was essentially a brilliant synthesis of researches which had been initiated by

1. See Black and Chrystal, *Life of William Robertson Smith*, pp. 383-403.
2. According to later editions, the first edition was published in April 1881, but Black and Chrystal (*Life of William Robertson Smith*, p. 416) say that it was published 'in the beginning of May'.
3. J. Wellhausen, *Geschichte Israels* (Berlin, 1878). The better known *Prolegomena zur Geschichte Israels* (Berlin, 1883) is a lightly revised version of the 1878 volume.

W.M.L. de Wette in 1806, and which had been taken up by others in two great bursts, from 1820–35, and 1865–78.[4] British reviews of these researches, and in one or two cases translations into English of works that embodied them, had appeared in Britain since the 1830s. It would not have been impossible for anyone who wanted to know what was happening in Continental critical scholarship, and who did not read German and Dutch, to piece together some of the elements used by Wellhausen in his synthesis.[5] The main likely impact upon anyone interested in critical scholarship would have been made, however, by the major critical works in English and English translation that were published from the 1860s. Chief among them were J.W. Colenso's volumes entitled *The Pentateuch and Joshua*, M. Kalisch's commentary on Leviticus, and the translations into English of Ewald's *History of Israel* and Kuenen's *The Religion of Israel*. I shall consider these briefly, together with Robertson Smith's ill-fated article 'Bible' in the *Encyclopaedia Britannica* as a yardstick against which to measure *The Old Testament in the Jewish Church*.

J.W. Colenso's *The Pentateuch and Joshua* appeared in seven parts between 1862 and 1879 and amounted to some 3500 pages.[6] As it progressed, its positions were modified in accordance with Colenso's own researches and with developments in Continental European criticism. The most important volume was Part VI, which argued that the levitical legislation (which Colenso found in Exodus, Numbers and Joshua as well as in Leviticus) was written after the exile. Further, noting the similarities between Ezekiel and the so-called Holiness Code of Leviticus 18–27, Colenso argued that Ezekiel had written chs. 18–20 and 26 of Leviticus during the exile. In previous volumes Colenso had closely studied the vocabulary of Deuteronomy and had identified Deuteronomic additions to the stories of the exodus, conquest and judges. Deuteronomy itself was assigned by him to the seventh century, with Jeremiah identified as the likely author. The main difference between Colenso's position and that of Wellhausen was that Colenso held that the *narratives* of what we today call P were early (the time of Samuel and David) while the *laws* were late (post-exilic), whereas Wellhausen regarded P as a whole as post-exilic. In this, Colenso was

---

4.   See Rogerson, *Old Testament Criticism.*
5.   For further details see Rogerson, *Old Testament Criticism*, ch. 12.
6.   J.W. Colenso, *The Pentateuch and Joshua Critically Examined* (7 parts; London, 1862–79). See Rogerson, *Old Testament Criticism*, ch. 16.

representative of the criticism of the time, and, in any case, admitted that he might be wrong about the early date of the narratives.

The likely impact of Colenso's work on his potential readers was blunted by three factors. First, Part I and the second volume of Part IV were devastatingly irreverent, since they pointed out the impossibilities of the literal reading of the stories of the crossing of the Red Sea and Noah's Ark. Secondly, Colenso, being a bishop, was held to have betrayed his office by raising critical questions. If an Anglican bishop could be criticised in the 1980s for raising critical questions, it does not require much imagination to see what a scandal this was in the 1860s! Thirdly, Colenso presented his arguments in great critical detail. If there is anything alien to the English (as opposed to the Scottish) character, it is that English people should be expected to apply themselves to hard intellectual work. What the English demand and require is ready-made answers. Colenso expected far too much of his compatriots!

Kalisch, a German Jew who sought refuge in Britain after the upheavals of 1848 in Germany, published his commentary on Leviticus in two parts, in 1867 and 1872.[7] In a remarkable way it anticipated Wellhausen's position of 1878. Kalisch argued that the levitical ordinances were neither known nor carried out before the exile, and that the minuteness of the sacrificial ritual in Leviticus accorded perfectly with the spirit of post-Babylonian times. He contrasted the dominant position of the priests in the levitical law with their total lack of importance in the history of ancient Israel as presented elsewhere in the Bible. He concluded that the priestly and levitical power was not in place from the time of Moses, but grew gradually over time, coming into its own only after the exile. As with Colenso so, probably, with Kalisch, the effect of these views was blunted because they were presented in the context of a commentary that required careful attention to minute details.

Ewald's *History of Israel,* whose translation into English began to appear in 1876 thanks to the efforts of Charlotte Lupton (who effaced herself from the project), was a step backwards.[8] Although it was critical—it treated the stories of Abraham, Isaac and Jacob as

---

7. M.M. Kalisch, *A Historical and Critical Commentary on the Old Testament with a New Translation. Leviticus* (Parts I and II; London, 1867–1872). See Rogerson, *Old Testament Criticism,* pp. 242-44.

8. H. Ewald, *Geschichte des Volkes Israel* (Göttingen, 1843–59); ET *History of Israel* (London, 1867–86). See Rogerson, *Old Testament Criticism,* pp. 91-103.

information about the interactions of groups rather than of individuals and was based upon source-critical research—it assigned a much more positive role to Moses and the priesthood than did the tradition of criticism that culminated in Wellhausen. For British purposes, it enabled moderate acceptance of biblical criticism to be combined with a traditional view of the history of Israelite religion, one essentially similar to that given in the Old Testament. Indeed, the existence of Ewald's position polarized those in Britain who were open to biblical criticism between the moderate critical but essentially traditional approach of Ewald and the radical approach which culminated in Wellhausen.

Kuenen's *The Religion of Israel*, whose English translation began to appear in 1874, was not only in the stream that led to Wellhausen, but was one of its most important sources. Its starting point was the eighth century, the earliest period for which Kuenen believed that there was sufficient evidence for writing history; but as he conjecturally worked back to earlier times, and although he allowed a positive, if moderate place for the work of Moses, he firmly rejected the idea that the priesthood in Solomon's temple was the levitical priesthood described in Leviticus and elsewhere. Further, he maintained that at the time of Ezekiel, no written ritual legislation existed, and he attributed the compilation of this, together with the final redaction of the Torah, to Ezra, who worked on this task in consultation with the priests in Jerusalem between the years 458 and 444. Thus Kuenen's account was one of the gradual development of Israel from a time in the early monarchy when every male Israelite could offer sacrifice, and when there were many Israelite sanctuaries, to the post-exilic situation when Jerusalem alone was the legitimate sanctuary, presided over by priests who alone could offer sacrifice.

The final writing to be considered as an antecedent to Smith's *Old Testament in the Jewish Church* is his own article 'Bible', which was published in December 1875 having been written in the middle of the same year. In this article, Smith distinguished three main sources which ran through the Pentateuch and Joshua: a Levitico-Elohistic document (what we today call P); a Jehovistic narrative which, beginning with the creation, treated the early history 'more in the spirit of prophetic theology and idealism'; and a third author 'belonging to northern Israel, and specially interested in the ancestors of the northern tribes' (E). Smith associated these three sources with 'three currents of interest' that he believed determined the course of Israelite history: 'the traditional lore of the priests, the teaching of the prophets, and the religious life of the more enlightened of the people'. After the book of Joshua, the Levitico-Elohistic source disappeared, possibly leaving the other two to run on as far as the books of Kings. The whole from Genesis to Kings had then been edited by a Deuteronomistic hand. The arguments for placing Deuteronomy no earlier than the seventh century were briefly rehearsed.

What is noteworthy about the article 'Bible' is that Smith left open the question whether the Levitico-Elohistic document was earlier or later than Deuteronomy. If it was later, then the system in which priests were superior to levites was the culmination of the development of the Israelite cult. If the Levitico-Elohistic document was earlier than Deuteronomy then its provisions existed as a legal programme 'long before the exile' even if the programme was not fully carried out until after Ezra. As Smith hinted, 'The solution of this problem has issues of the greatest importance for the theology as well as for the literary history of the Old Testament'. By the time that he delivered the lectures that became *The Old Testament in the Jewish Church* Smith had decided in favour of the view that the Levitico-Elohistic document was the latest of the three, and he had reconstructed the literary history of the Old Testament accordingly. In this he was no doubt helped by Wellhausen's *Geschichte Israels* of 1878, which he described as the most important book on the subject.[9] Yet, in laying out the position as he now saw it, Smith did not merely repeat the arguments of Wellhausen, or anyone else; he approached the subject in a quite original way.[10]

Before I describe this, I must remind you that the account of Israel's religious and literary history comes at the *end* of *The Old Testament in the Jewish Church* and that it is preceded by chapters dealing with the text and canon of the Old Testament, and a chapter on the Psalms. Yet, for strategic reasons, I shall concentrate on the last five of the twelve lectures. Not only did they concern the central issue of critical scholarship of the time; they foreshadowed Smith's later work on Semitic religion and sacrifice, and were vital to Smith's belief that the critical

---

9. Smith, *Old Testament in the Jewish Church*, p. 418 n. 1.

10. Smith's view of Wellhausen's *Geschichte* was that it had not said anything new but had worked 'the scattered data into a consistent and intelligible historical picture more complete than anything that has been hitherto attempted'. See Smith, Review of Wellhausen, in *Lectures and Essays*, pp. 601-607.

views that he was advocating were necessary for the maintenance of evangelical Christian faith.

Lecture VIII is entitled 'The Traditional Theory of the Old Testament History' and begins by setting out the implications of the view that the whole levitical system of sacrifice and priesthood was instituted by Moses. Smith describes the system as 'a complete theory of the religious life', and emphasizes that it did not only deal with *where* God should be worshipped, but *how*.[11] Under this latter heading, God was so awesome in his holiness that access to him could only be via a priest. His sanctuary or its vessels could not be touched without danger by unqualified people; and the lives of the people were regulated by rules about ritual holiness, the violation of which required remedy by the offering of sacrifice. Under this dispensation,

> the mass of the people have no direct access to their God in the sanctuary. The maintenance of the Old Testament covenant depends on the priestly mediation, and above all on that one annual day of expiation when the High Priest enters the Holy of Holies.[12]

Smith points out that this view of the levitical legislation as being a complete theory of religious life passed into Christianity, with the modification that the system was no longer regarded as God's final word. That final word was in the atonement made possible by Christ; but the levitical system had once been God's means of grace, and it pointed, typically, to the sacrifice of Christ.

Against the levitical theory of religion Smith juxtaposed the popular religion of Israel as described from the book of Judges onwards. He reminded his hearers and readers of the difference between worship as understood by Christians, and worship as part of the life of the ordinary Israelite:

> To us worship is a spiritual thing. We lift up our hearts and voices to God in the closet, the family, or the church, persuaded that God, who is spirit, will receive in every place the worship of spirit and truth...Under the Old Testament it was otherwise...the Old Testament worshipper sought access to his God in an earthly sanctuary which was for him, as it were, the meeting place of heaven and earth.[13]

There then follows a vivid picture, drawn from the Old Testament, of

---

11. *Old Testament in the Jewish Church*, p. 212.
12. *Old Testament in the Jewish Church*, p. 211.
13. *Old Testament in the Jewish Church*, pp. 223-24.

the practical meaning of worship for ordinary Israelites, a practical worship centred on the sanctuary, which no worshipper would ever enter without bringing a gift. Furthermore, no ordinary Israelite would think of praying to God anywhere other than the sanctuary.

Smith admits that the worship offered by ordinary Israelites was not above criticism. It could confuse the God of Israel with the Canaanite gods. The popular sanctuaries at which Israelites worshipped were originally Canaanite sanctuaries and retained Canaanite practices. From the standpoint of the prophets popular religion could be described as disloyalty to the God of Israel. But now Smith makes a startling claim, which is that whatever anyone else might have thought, ordinary Israelites themselves would have seen things differently.

> They still believed themselves loyal to Jehovah. Their great sanctuaries were patriarchal holy places like Bethel, and Beersheba, or purely Hebrew foundations like Dan.[14]

Smith goes on to point out that, for all its corruptions, their worship was the worship of their national God, and to that extent stood in the Mosaic tradition. Smith does not at this point claim that Israel's popular worship was, for the worshippers, authentic intercourse with the God of grace; he prefers to develop his argument along different lines, as we shall see shortly. But he ends Lecture VIII with a striking contrast between the two religions, the levitical and the popular, which deserves partial quotation. Of the levitical religion:

> The access of the ordinary Israelite to God is very restricted. He can only stand afar off while the priest approaches Jehovah as his mediator, and brings back a word of blessing. And even this mediate access to God is confined to his visits to the central sanctuary...Other sanctuaries are not simply less holy, places of less solemn tryst with Jehovah; they are places where His holiness is not revealed, and therefore are not, and cannot be, sanctuaries of Jehovah at all.[15]

Of the popular religion:

> Opportunity of access to Jehovah is near to every Israelite, and every occasion of life that calls on the individual, the clan, or the village, to look Godwards is a summons to the altar. In the family every feast was an eucharistic sacrifice...The earlier history relates scarcely one event of importance that was not transacted at a holy place. The local sanctuaries

---

14. *Old Testament in the Jewish Church*, p. 231.
15. *Old Testament in the Jewish Church*, p. 234.

were the centres of all Hebrew life. How little of the history would remain
if Shechem and Bethel, the two Mizpahs and Ophra, Gilgal, Ramah, and
Gibeon, Hebron, Bethlehem, and Beersheba, Kadesh, and Mahanaim,
Tabor and Carmel, were blotted out of the pages of the Old Testament! [16]

In spite of this devastating rhetoric, Smith did not feel that he had
proved his point. He had much more ammunition and did not want to
break off the battle at this point! He graciously admits that the contrast
he has just drawn between the popular and the levitical religion can be
accommodated to the traditional view that the levitical religion is Mosaic
if the popular religion provided no true access to God. One might
sustain this for the popular religion of unnamed Israelites. It cannot be
sustained in the case of figures such as Samuel and David.

Lecture IX confronts the levitical theory not with popular religion, but
with the religion of figures such as Samuel, and with the practice of the
First Temple prior to the exile, in an attempt to show that the levitical
legislation was not known in the pre-exilic period. Thus, Smith saw no
difference between the two brazen pillars which stood at the porch of
Solomon's temple and the *matstsevot* forbidden by Deut. 16.21 and
Lev. 26.1. He also pointed out that whereas Num. 3.38 forbids any
foreigner (*zar*) to approach the sanctuary on pain of death, the First
Temple was actually policed by a royal bodyguard of foreign
mercenaries, the Kerethim and Pelethim, who were probably Cretans
and Philistines. Smith reminds readers and listeners of the part played by
the foreign bodyguard on the installation as king of the boy Jehoash in
2 Kings 11.

Another example, of which Smith makes much, is the temple at
Shiloh. If there was any sanctuary in Israel that was a legitimate sanctuary before the Jerusalem temple was built, then it was Shiloh. In Jer.
7.12 it is described as the place where God set his name first. It contained the ark and it was served by a priesthood to whose ancestor the
LORD had revealed himself in Egypt, according to 1 Sam. 2.27-8. If
there was any sanctuary where details of the ritual instituted by Moses
were preserved, then it was here in Shiloh.

And yet, as Smith points out, the considerable information given in
the opening chapters of 1 Samuel about the ritual arrangements at
Shiloh indicates that practice there was at variance with the levitical
legislation. Thus the sons of the priest Eli are criticized because they
would not burn the fat of sacrifices until they had been given a portion

16. *Old Testament in the Jewish Church*, p. 235.

of the uncooked meat (1 Sam. 2.12-17). When they took this by force, they are described as having treated the offerings of the LORD with contempt. Yet according to Lev. 7.30-31 it was required that the priest should have a part of the flesh when he turned the fat into smoke on the altar. Again, the ark was not secluded from every eye in the Shiloh temple, but stood in a building whose doors were opened daily. As Smith remarks, the Day of Atonement could not legitimately have been performed at the Shiloh sanctuary.[17] Furthermore, one of the ministers at Shiloh, Samuel, did not even come from a priestly family. It is true that his mother had dedicated him to the service of God; but this, from the point of view of the levitical legislation, could not make him a priest. Only someone born of a priestly family could be a priest.

Samuel's subsequent conduct was also inconsistent with the levitical legislation in that he offered sacrifice at various places after the destruction of Shiloh by the Philistines, and made no attempt to bring together, for example, the priestly family of Eli who where the guardians of the Ark of the Covenant and who went to Nob, and the Ark itself that was at Kiriath-jearim. As Smith remarks, 'Samuel did not know of a systematic and exclusive system of sacrificial ritual confined to the sanctuary of the ark'; and he concluded,

> Grant with Jeremiah that sacrifice is a free expression of Israel's homage which Jehovah has not yet regulated by law, and at once the conduct of Samuel is clear, and Jehovah's acceptance of his service intelligible.[18]

Lecture X is entitled 'The Prophets' and contributes to Smith's overall arguments in the following ways. First, he emphasizes the great difference between the prophetic view of God's relationship with Israel and the view implied in the levitical legislation. The awesome, unapproachable God of the latter is contrasted with the God who, in prophetic imagery, is described as having a tender, intimate relationship with his people. The centrality of sacrifice as the way to approach God in the levitical legislation is contrasted with the prophetic denunciations of sacrifice, and with statements such as those in Amos 5.25 and Jer. 7.22 that God did not require sacrifices from Israel when they were in the wilderness in the exile. Secondly, he argues that the mission of the prophets can only be understood as preparing the way for the levitical legislation, and certainly not as shaped by a levitical legislation in place

17. *Old Testament in the Jewish Church*, p. 259.
18. *Old Testament in the Jewish Church*, p. 263.

from the time of Moses. The task of the prophets was to lead the people away from a conception of God that hardly differed from the conceptions of their gods entertained by Israel's heathen neighbours. Ordinary Israelites, like their Moabite and Ammonite neighbours, wanted a national god who would serve their interests and, through divination, would help them cope with the uncertainties of life. The God of the Israelite prophets was altogether different. He had chosen his people to serve his purposes, and not vice versa, and through the vicissitudes of their history wished to impart moral values that would set the people apart from their neighbours. Thirdly, Smith's discussion of the prophets underlined his theological agenda. The prophets were not merely acute observers of their world. They were inspired people who had a close relationship with God and who, out of this relationship, exercised a ministry of grace to the people. If their work pointed to the coming of Christ it was not because they were predictors of the future, but because they had a profound belief in what God intended his people to become.

Smith's remaining task, in the two final lectures, was to account for the writing of the Pentateuch, and to correlate this process with the history of Israelite religion as he had begun to reconstruct it. He did so by distinguishing three collections of laws, Exodus 21–23 (which he called the First Legislation), Deuteronomy 12–26 (the Deuteronomic Code) and the levitical legislation, scattered through Exodus, Leviticus and Numbers. He then described the 'social system adapted for a very definite national life' implied in the First Legislation.[19]

There is presented a vivid picture of a simple agricultural society whose property laws deal almost exclusively with cattle and agricultural produce, and whose civil and criminal justice is based upon principles 'still current among the Arabs of the desert'.[20]

The individual Israelite is a person of 'independent bearing and personal dignity', there is no strong central authority, and practices such as blood revenge regulate murder and personal injuries. The Sabbath exists to prevent exploitation and the poor are provided for by letting them enjoy the produce of sabbatical years. Firstlings and first fruits must be presented to God at the sanctuary, and the whole system implies a plurality of sanctuaries. Smith emphasizes that this legislation and its worship has much in common with the legislation of other nations. Yet there is an emerging distinctiveness in that the God of Israel is believed to have

19. *Old Testament in the Jewish Church*, p. 328.
20. *Old Testament in the Jewish Church*, p. 336.

delivered his people from slavery in Egypt, and his favour is directed by moral principles, and not a natural relationship.

Yet for all its dignity and the possibility that it offered for a religion of spontaneous joy, the First Legislation could not guarantee that Israel's religion would not degenerate into the heathenism of its neighbours. The prophetic condemnations of such degeneration, and their call to a higher morality and religion, needed to be given legislative form. This was the purpose of the Deuteronomic Code which, by insisting on only one sanctuary, was designed to prevent the assimilation of Israel's religion to that of its neighbours. As the basis for Josiah's reformation in 622 it enjoyed only a brief period of effectiveness before Josiah's death, and then the fall of Jerusalem altered the situation radically. In this new situation it was Ezekiel who provided the impetus for the various teachings about ritual and sacrifice preserved by the priests to be formed into the levitical legislation. The levites were degraded into inferior ministers, provision was made for regular offerings as part of the daily worship, and prominence was given to the sin offering and atoning ritual. This process of redefining the place of the temple, sacrifice and priesthood in Israel's religion lasted until Ezra; and as this religion concentrated ever more on the difficulty of access to God for ordinary worshippers, so there developed new forms of spiritual, non-ritual religion, in the tradition of the prophets and as expressed in the Psalms. The setting for this non-ritual religion was the synagogue.

At this point it would have been understandable if Smith had made the value judgment that we find in some of his contemporaries, and which suited some types of Christian apologetic, namely, that the levitical legislation marked the decline of Old Testament religion into Judaism, and that the spiritual and ethical religion of the prophets was the high point. In fact, Smith assessed the levitical legislation positively:

> It did not bring Israel into such direct converse with Jehovah as prophecy had done. But for the mass of the people it nevertheless formed a distinct step in advance, for it put an end to the anomalous state of things in which practical heathenism had filled the state, and the prophets preached to deaf ears. The legal ritual did not satisfy the highest spiritual needs, but it practically extinguished idolatry. It gave palpable expression to the spiritual nature of Jehovah, and, around and within the ritual, prophetic truths gained a hold of Israel such as they never had before. [21]

I have devoted many pages to describing five of Smith's twelve

---

21. *Old Testament in the Jewish Church*, pp. 313-14.

lectures. Before I discuss their impact and importance I must devote a couple of paragraphs to the first seven lectures! Of these, five are about the text, versions and canon of the Old Testament; and while they no doubt made considerable demands on their original hearers, Smith adopted an approach that was certainly designed to hold their attention. He began with the English version of the Old Testament familiar to his readers, and raised a number of questions that are unfailingly of interest to any non-specialist who takes the Bible seriously: on what manuscripts is the English translation based, how and when were the manuscripts copied, what relation do they bear to what the biblical writers wrote, how did the biblical writers write and how and when did these writings come to be regarded as Scripture? By pressing these questions Smith was able to discuss the importance of the ancient versions of the Old Testament, especially the Septuagint, to discuss scribal techniques and, above all, to make the important point that in ancient Israel the functions of author, editor and scribe merged together in a way unfamiliar to us. The results gained from these lectures were then taken to the Psalms where, again, questions were pressed that are of general interest: who wrote the Psalms and when, what do the titles mean, how were the Psalms collected together and divided into five books?

The implications of the answers provided to the many questions raised were no doubt radical for Smith's hearers and first readers. The traditional Hebrew text upon which English translations were based was only one witness to what the biblical authors wrote, and it was not always the most reliable witness. The processes of writing, editing and copying were human, understandable processes, even if they were different from how we understand these tasks. The Psalms were composed and collected together over a period of at least five hundred years, and the titles which ascribed many of them to David and put some of them into the context of incidents in his life were not reliable guides to their authorship or interpretation.

Smith's strategy in all this was no doubt to undermine approaches to the Old Testament that saw its text as a supernatural phenomenon, whose authors had been passive instruments through whom God had dictated, and whose autographs had been providentially preserved from mistakes in the copying process. His insistence all along was that the historical study of the origins and textual transmission of the Bible was an enterprise that embodied the principles of the Reformation. Further, the lectures were delivered not in a negative spirit, but in a manner dominated by the excitement of discovery, discovery that released rather than diminished the power of the Old Testament for Smith's world. The following statement is representative:

> the Psalter and the Old Testament in general are to us not merely books of devotion but sources of study for the better knowledge of the whole course of God's revelation. It is a law of all science that, to know a thing thoroughly, we must understand it in its genesis and in its growth. To understand the ways of God with man, and the whole meaning of His plan of salvation, it is necessary to go back and see His work in its beginnings, examining the rudimentary stages of the process of revelation; and for this the Psalms are invaluable, for they give us the first answer of the believing heart to God under a dispensation where the objective elements of revelation were far less fully developed, and where spiritual processes were in many respects more naive and childlike.[22]

This brings me to a comparison of Smith with his great contemporaries. Kuenen and Wellhausen were historians and not theologians. Their concern was to advance the truth, all the more so if they were opposed by theological interests that regarded the truth as a threat to traditional orthodoxy. Smith, too, was a historian, and shared the concern that truth should triumph over prejudice. But it cannot be stressed too strongly that Smith was *not* a compromiser, or someone who accepted the results of criticism reluctantly, and accommodated them to an increasingly watered-down version of Christianity. On the contrary, Smith was an enthusiast for biblical criticism because he believed that it freed the Old Testament from fetters that made it a closed book. Whereas traditional orthodoxy, when faced with the words, 'the LORD spoke to Moses', was concerned to defend at all costs the last two words 'to Moses', thereby insisting on an approach to the Old Testament that became a stumbling block to the faith of any intelligent or sensitive reader, Smith fastened on the words 'the LORD spoke'.[23] With the help of criticism these words took on new meaning, and the Old Testament could be used to write a history of grace, recording God's successive acts of grace to his people adapted to the quite different situations of an unfolding history. And for Smith, the God whose history of grace was disclosed by the historical criticism of the Old Testament was the God whose grace was still offered to the human race.

Interestingly enough, it was the overtly theological tone of Smith's

---

22. *Old Testament in the Jewish Church*, pp. 180-81.
23. *Old Testament in the Jewish Church*, p. 306.

lectures that disturbed some of Smith's reviewers. Black and Chrystal quote Cheyne as follows:

> It would be a pity if any one…should be repelled from the study of the work by its ultra-Protestant tendencies, a pity moreover were it to be demanded of every Old Testament scholar that he should be always holding up his theological flag.[24]

Yet arguably this misses the point, and fails to see how vital biblical criticism was to Smith as part of the church's mission. Cheyne was nearer the mark in saying that the *Old Testament in the Jewish Church* would lay a firm foundation for the study of biblical criticism in Britain.

In 1892 Smith published a second and revised edition of the book. The main differences between the two editions are as follows. First, the endnotes of the first edition become updated footnotes in the second edition. Secondly, there is an additional chapter that reflects on the chapters dealing with the law and on recent scholarship; there are also some Additional Notes. Thirdly, within the main body of the text the substantial alterations are to sections on the text and canon, and on the Psalter, where the dates of the collections are brought lower than in the first edition. The opening chapter, with its passionate appeal to the Reformation, and the five chapters dealing with the history of the law are left virtually unaltered. Only a section on the Mosaic authorship of the Pentateuch and reasons for rejecting it is enlarged. The argument as a whole is untouched.

Indications of the influence of the two editions can only be in the nature of random samples. There are three references to the first edition in the preface to A.F. Kirkpatrick's commentary on the Psalms,[25] while in R.L. Ottley's Bampton Lectures of 1897 *Aspects of the Old Testament*, seven of the twelve references to Smith's work are from *The Old Testament in the Jewish Church*.[26] Arthur S. Peake describes, in his essay on Robertson Smith, how the second edition helped his development, especially its discussion of the Protestant doctrine of Scripture,[27] while in his book *The Bible: Its Origin, its Significance and its Abiding*

---

24. Black and Chrystal, *Life of William Robertson Smith*, p. 419.

25. A.F. Kirkpatrick, *The Book of Psalms* (Cambridge Bible for Schools and Colleges; Cambridge, 1891). See pp. xii, xxvi, xlvii.

26. R.L. Ottley, *Aspects of the Old Testament* (London, 1897). See pp. 8, 49, 94, 122, 138, 242, 283.

27. A.S. Peake, *Recollections and Appreciations* (ed. W.F. Howard; London: Epworth Press, 1938), p. 92.

Worth Peake defended the 'legitimacy and necessity' of biblical criticism by quoting the following passage from Smith:

> If in the application you find me calling in a rationalistic principle, if you can show at any step in my argument that I assume the impossibility of the supernatural or reject plain fact in the interests of rationalistic theories, I will frankly confess that I am in the wrong.[28]

What, then, of the book's abiding value? I select three items. First, I find it astonishing that one hundred years after Smith's death we are still dependent on English translations of the Bible that take the traditional Hebrew text as their basis, and depart from it only when it is corrupt or there is strong evidence against it. The differences of order and of text in Jeremiah between the Massoretic and the Septuagint tradition, of which Smith made such effective use in his arguments,[29] are not indicated by modern translations. A critical translation based upon an eclectic text would assist readers to move beyond naive literalism. Secondly, Smith's method of arguing for the 'Wellhausen position' still has great value. A recent distinguished commentary on Leviticus suggests that the priestly legislation originated from Shiloh, and it would be interesting to compare its arguments with those of Smith, who took the opposite view.[30] Thirdly, Smith's insistence that biblical criticism is essential for Christian belief needs to be recovered. Not only do we witness today a fear in churches of critical thought and a flourishing of types of fundamentalism; we also hear in some academic circles that only those without a religious commitment can be trusted to study the Bible objectively.

But let the last word on *The Old Testament in the Jewish Church* be left to his great disciple Stanley A. Cook who described it, in his book *The 'Truth' of the Bible*, as 'the most original and, from the religious point of view, the most persuasive exposition and justification of the

---

28. A.S. Peake, *The Bible: Its Origin, its Significance, and its Abiding Worth* (London: Hodder & Stoughton, 1913), p. 96.

29. See *Jewish Church*, pp. 113-14, where Smith prints out a translation of Jer. 27.5-22 with the passages common to the Greek and Hebrew versions in roman type and the additional passages that appear in the Hebrew only in italics. This indicates that, while the Greek version does not envisage the return of the temple vessels to Jerusalem, the Hebrew version does. According to Smith, if we accept the Greek version as the more original 'we remove a serious inconsistency from [Jeremiah's] religious teaching' (p. 117).

30. J. Milgrom, *Leviticus 1–16: A New Translation with Introduction and Commentary* (AB, 3; Garden City, NY: Doubleday, 1991), pp. 13-34.

"Wellhausen hypothesis"'.[31] And Cook summed up Smith's whole work in the service of biblical criticism and Christian faith in the following words:

> The seeds sown by Robertson Smith still bear fruit, and his combination of unequalled knowledge and simple faith is as a beacon-light to those who fear that the harmonious adjustment of the claims of Religion and Research is no longer attainable. On his tombstone in the little village of Keig are engraved the words of Psalm xxv. 14: 'The secret of the Lord is with them that fear Him'—challenging words, if true, and, like the motto of his old University: Initium Sapientiae Timor Domini, a fine devotional sentiment to be respectfully left with those who can believe in them...[32]

31. Cook, *'Truth'*, p. 16.
32. Cook, *'Truth'*, p. xv.

BIBLIOGRAPHY

Albright, W.F., *From the Stone Age to Christianity* (Garden City, NY: Doubleday, 2nd edn, 1957).

Alt, A, 'Der Gott der Väter', in *Kleine Schriften zur Geschichte des Volkes Israel* (Munich: Beck, 1959), I, pp. 1-78.

Bailey, W.M., 'Theology and Criticism in William Robertson Smith' (PhD dissertation, Yale University, 1970).

Baumgartner, H.M., *Kontinuität und Geschichte: Zur Kritik und Metakritik der historischen Vernunft* (Frankfurt: Suhrkamp, 1972).

Begg, J., *Happy Homes for Working Men, and How to Get Them* (London, 1866).

Beidelman, T.O., *W. Robertson Smith and the Sociological Study of Religion* (Chicago: University of Chicago Press, 1974).

Black, J.S., and G. Chrystal, *The Life of William Robertson Smith* (London: A. & C. Black, 1912).

Bright, J., *A History of Israel* (London: SCM Press, 1961).

Brown, T., *Annals of the Disruption; with Extracts from the Narratives of Ministers who left the Scottish Establishment in 1843* (Edinburgh, 1884).

Bryce, J., *Studies in Contemporary Biography* (New York: Macmillan, 1903).

Carroll, R.P., *From Chaos to Covenant: Uses of Prophecy in the Book of Jeremiah* (London: SCM Press, 1981).

Carswell, D., *Brother Scots* (London: Constable, 2nd impression, 1927).

Clarke, A., *The Holy Bible with a Commentary and Critical Notes* (London, 1825).

Clements, R.E., 'George Stanley Faber (1773–1854) as Biblical Interpreter', in P. Mommer and W. Thiel (eds.), *Altes Testament, Forschung und Wirkung: Festschrift für Henning Graf Reventlow* (Frankfurt: Peter Lang, 1994), pp. 247-68.

Clines, D.J.A., *The Theme of the Pentateuch* (JSOTSup, 10; Sheffield: JSOT Press, 1979).

Colenso, J.W., *The Pentateuch and Joshua Critically Examined* (7 parts; London, 1862–79).

Cook, S.A., *The 'Truth' of the Bible* (Cambridge: Heffer; London: SPCK; New York: Macmillan, 1938).

Danto, A.C., *An Analytical Philosophy of History* (Cambridge: Cambridge University Press, 1965).

Dibelius, O., *Das Königliche Predigerseminar zu Wittenberg 1817–1917* (Berlin-Lichterfeld: Varlag von Edwin Runge, n.d.)

Eichrodt, W., *Old Testament Theology* (London: SCM Press, 1962).

Eliot, G., *Middlemarch* (The Penguin English Library; Harmondsworth: Penguin, 1965).

Esslinger, L. *et al.* (eds.), *Ascribe to the Lord: Essays in Memory of Peter C. Craigie* (JSOTSup, 67; Sheffield: JSOT Press, 1988).

Ewald, H., *Die Propheten des Alten Bundes* (Göttingen, 1866).

—*Geschichte des Volkes Israel* (Göttingen, 1843–59); ET *History of Israel* (London, 1867–86).

Flegg, C.G., *'Gathered under Apostles': A Study of the Catholic Apostolic Church* (Oxford: Clarendon Press, 1992).

Gerstenberger, E., *Psalms, Part 1* (FOTL, 14; Grand Rapids: Eerdmans, 1988).

Giddens, A., and J. Turner (eds.), *Social Theory Today* (Cambridge: Polity Press, 1987).

Graf, F.W., 'Kulturprotestantismus', in *TRE*, XX (Berlin: de Gruyter, 1990), pp. 230-43.

Gunkel, H., *Die Psalmen übersetzt und erklärt* (HAT; Göttingen: Vandenhoeck & Ruprecht, 4th edn, 1926).

Hanhart, R., 'Paul Anton de Lagarde und seine Kritik an der Theologie', in B. Moeller (ed.), *Theologie in Göttingen: Eine Vorlesungsreihe* (Göttinger Universitätsschriften Series A, 1; Göttingen: Vandenhoek & Ruprecht, 1987), pp. 271-305.

Hausrath, A., *Richard Rothe und seine Freunde* (Berlin: Grote'sche Verlagsbuchhandlung, 1902–1906).

Hirsch, E., *Geschichte der neuern evangelischen Theologie* (Gütersloh: Gerd Mohn, 3rd edn, 1964).

Horne, T.H., *An Introduction to the Critical Study and Knowledge of the Holy Scriptures* (London, 10th edn, 1859).

Houtman, C., 'William Robertson Smith (1846–1894): His Life and Work in the Light of his Correspondence with Abraham Kuenen', in J. Bremmer and H. Kippenberg (eds.), *The Rise of the Science of Religion in the Nineteenth Century: A Biographical Approach* (Supplements to *Numen*; Leiden: Brill, forthcoming).

Hutchison, J.G.C., *A Political History of Scotland 1832–1924: Parties, Elections and Issues* (Edinburgh: John Donald, 1986).

Johnson, A.R., *Sacral Kingship in Ancient Israel* (Cardiff: University of Wales Press, 2nd edn, 1967).

Kalisch, M.M., *A Historical and Critical Commentary on the Old Testament with a New Translation: Leviticus* (London, 1867–1872).

Kirkpatrick, A.F., *The Book of Psalms* (Cambridge Bible for Schools and Colleges; Cambridge, 1891).

Kuenen, A., *De godsdienst van Israël tot den ondergang van der Joodschen staat*, II (Haarlem, 1870); trans. by A.H. May as *The Religion of Israel to the Fall of the Jewish State* (London, 1875).

Lagrange, M.-J., *Personal Reflections and Memoirs* (New York: Paulist Press, 1985).

Lotze, H., *Microcosmos: An Essay concerning Man and his Relation to the World* (2 vols.; Edinburgh, 1897).

Lewes, G.H., *The Life and Works of Goethe* (London, 1855).

Maurice, F., *The Life of Frederick Denison Maurice Chiefly Told in his Own Letters* (London, 1884).

Maurice, F.D., *Theological Essays* (Cambridge, 1853).

—*The Doctrine of Sacrifice Deduced from the Scriptures* (Cambridge, 1854).

—*The Prophets and Kings of the Old Testament* (London, 1879).

—*The Patriarchs and Lawgivers of the Old Testament* (London, 1892).

—*The Kingdom of Christ* (2 vols.; repr.; London: James Clarke, 2nd edn, 1959 [1842]).

—*The Prayer Book* (London: James Clarke, 3rd edn 1966).

McCobb, A., *George Eliot's Knowledge of German Life and Letters* (Salzburg Studies in English Literature, Romantic Reassessment, 102.2; Salzburg: Institut für Anglistik und Americanistik der Universität Salzburg, 1982).

Mechie, S., *The Church and Scottish Social Development 1780–1870* (London: Oxford University Press, 1960).

Milgrom, J., *Leviticus 1–16: A New Translation with Introduction and Commentary* (AB, 3; Garden City, NY: Doubleday, 1991).

Moore, J.R., 'Freethought, Secularism, Agnosticism: The Case of Charles Darwin', in G. Parsons (ed.) *Religion in Victorian Britain. I. Traditions* (Manchester: Manchester University Press, 1988), pp. 274-319.

Mowinckel, S., *The Psalms in Israel's Worship* (trans. D.R. Ap-Thomas; Oxford: Basil Blackwell, 1962).

Münch, R., *Die Struktur der Moderne: Grundmuster und differentielle Gestaltung des institutionelle Aufbaus der modernen Gesellschaften* (Frankfurt: Suhrkamp, 1984).

—*Die Kultur der Moderne. I. Ihre Grundlagen und ihre Entwicklung in England und Amerika* (Frankfurt: Suhrkamp, 1986).

—*Die Kultur der Moderne. II. Ihre Entwicklung in Frankreich und Deutschland* (Frankfurt: Suhrkamp, 1986).

Newman, F., *A History of the Hebrew Monarchy from the Administration of Samuel to the Babylonian Captivity* (London, 1847).

Ottley, R.L., *Aspects of the Old Testament* (London, 1897).

Pannenberg, W., 'Geschichte', VIII, 5, in *TRE* (1984), XII, pp. 667ff.

Peake, A.S., *The Bible: Its Origin, its Significance, and its Abiding Worth* (London: Hodder & Stoughton, 1913).

—*Recollections and Appreciations* (ed. W.F. Howard; London: Epworth Press, 1938).

Petersen, D., *The Roles of Israel's Prophets* (JSOTSup, 17; Sheffield: JSOT Press, 1981).

Prothero, R.E., and G.G. Bradley, *The Life and Correspondence of Arthur Penrhyn Stanley DD, Late Dean of Westminster* (London, 1893).

Rad, G. von, *Theologie des Alten Testaments. I. Die Theologie der geschichtlichen Traditionen* (Munich: Chr. Kaiser Verlag, 1961).

Raven, C.E., *Christian Socialism, 1848–1854* (London: Macmillan, 1920).

Rendtorff, R., 'Geschichte und Überlieferung', in *Gesammelte Studien zum Alten Testament* (Theologische Bücherei, Altes Testament, 57; Munich: Chr. Kaiser Verlag, 1975), pp. 25-38.

Ritschl, A., *Die christliche Lehre von der Rechtfertigung und Versöhnung*, III (Bonn, 1874); II (3rd edn, Bonn, 1889).

Ritschl, O., *Albrecht Ritschls Leben* (2 vols.; Freiburg im Breisgau, 1892–96).

Rogerson, J.W., *Myth in Old Testament Interpretation* (BZAW, 134; Berlin: de Gruyter, 1974).

—*Anthropology and the Old Testament* (Biblical Seminar, 1; repr.; Sheffield: JSOT Press, 1984 [1978]).

—*Old Testament Criticism in the Nineteenth Century, England and Germany* (London: SPCK, 1984).

—*W.M.L. de Wette, Founder of Modern Biblical Criticism: An Intellectual Biography* (JSOTSup, 126; Sheffield: JSOT Press, 1992).

Rothe, R., *Zur Dogmatik* (Von Neuem durchgesehener und durchgängig vermehter Abdruck aus den Theol. Studien und Kritiken, Gotha, 1863).

Simpson, P. Carnegie, *The Life of Principal Rainy* (London: Hodder & Stoughton, 1909).

Smend, R., *Deutsche Alttestamentler in drei Jahrhunderten* (Göttingen: Vandenhoeck & Ruprecht, 1989).

Smith, William, *Dictionary of the Bible* (London, 1863).

Smith, W.R., 'Prophecy in the Critical Schools of the Continent', *BQR* 51.102 (1870).

—'German and Dutch Periodicals', *BFE* 22 (1873), pp. 376-84.

—'Dutch and German Periodicals', *BFE* 23 (1874), pp. 176-82.

—'Bible', in *Encyclopaedia Britannica* (9th edn, 1875), III, p. 639.

—'The Progress of Old Testament Studies', *BFE* 25 (1876), pp. 471-93.

—'The Study of the Old Testament in 1876', *BEF* 26 (1877), pp. 779-805, reprinted in *Lectures and Essays*, pp. 367-99.

—*Sermon Preached in St George's Free Church, Edinburgh on the Afternoon of Sabbath, 27th May 1877* (Edinburgh, 1877).

—'Animal Worship and Animal Tribes among the Arabs and in the Old Testament', *Journal of Philology* 19 (1880), pp. 75-100; reprinted in *Lectures and Essays*, pp. 455-83.

—*The Old Testament in the Jewish Church: Twelve Lectures on Biblical Criticism* (Edinburgh, 1881).

—*The Prophets of Israel and their Place in History to the Close of the Eighth Century BC* (Edinburgh, 1882).

—*The Old Testament in the Jewish Church: A Course of Lectures on Biblical Criticism* (London, 2nd edn, 1892).

—*Lectures and Essays of William Robertson Smith* (ed. J.S. Black and G. Chrystal; London: A. & C. Black, 1912).

Smith, T., *Memoirs of James Begg, DD, Including Autobiographical Chapters by Dr Begg* (Edinburgh, 1885–88).

Steiner, G., *Real Presences: Is there Anything* in *What we Say?* (London: Faber & Faber, 1989).

Strahan, J., *Andrew Bruce Davidson* (London: Hodder & Stoughton, 1917).

Temple, F., 'The Education of the World', in *Essays and Reviews* (London, 5th edn, 1861), pp. 1-49.

Vidler, A.R., *F.D. Maurice and Company: Nineteenth-Century Studies* (London: SCM Press, 1966).

Wellhausen, J., *Der Text der Bücher Samuelis untersucht* (Göttingen, 1872).

—*Geschichte Israels* (Berlin, 1878).

Wette, W.M.L. de, *Beiträge zur Einleitung in das Alte Testament* (Halle, 1806–1807).

—*Lehrbuch der historisch-kritischen Einleitung in das Alte Testament* (Berlin, 7th edn, 1852).

White, J.F., *Two Professors of Oriental Languages* (Aberdeen, 1899).

Wilson, R.R., *Prophecy and Society in Ancient Israel* (Philadelphia: Fortress Press, 1980).

Wood, H.G., *Frederick Denison Maurice* (Cambridge: Cambridge University Press, 1950).

Wright, G.E., *God Who Acts: Biblical Theology as Recital* (SBT, 8; London: SCM Press, 1952).

—*Biblical Archaeology* (London: Duckworth; Philadelphia: Westminster Press, 2nd edn, 1962).

INDEXES

INDEX OF REFERENCES

OLD TESTAMENT

NEW TESTAMENT

CAMBRIDGE UNIVERSITY LIBRARY DOCUMENTS

INDEX OF AUTHORS

JOURNAL FOR THE STUDY OF THE OLD TESTAMENT

Supplement Series